AEC
Buses in camera

Cover transparency: C. R. Warn

Right: *West Bridgford UDC was a keen supporter of AEC until its all one make fleet of 38 buses was taken over by Nottingham City Transport in 1968. Three of the double-deckers were 61-seat Park Royal-bodied Regent Vs new in 1955 with AV470 engines.* Author's Collection

Overleaf: *Chester's first buses were AECs bought in 1930, and the make predominated until the outbreak of World War 2. This Regent is one of four placed in service in 1939 with Massey 54-seat bodies. It was withdrawn in 1953.* Author's Collection

AEC
Buses in camera

Robin Hannay

LONDON

IAN ALLAN LTD

First published 1982

ISBN 0 7110 1160 5

© Ian Allan Ltd 1982

Published by Ian Allan Ltd, Shepperton, Surrey;
and printed by Ian Allan Printing Ltd at their works
at Coombelands in Runnymede, England

Below: *With Caernarvon Castle in the background, this Cynnog and
Trevor AEC Regal started life in 1948 with Trent Motor Traction as
one of a batch of 43 carrying 35-seat Willowbrook half cab bodies.
In 1958 20 of the batch were rebuilt to full front by Willowbrook
and lengthened to accommodate four more passengers. They were
withdrawn in 1962.* Author's Collection

Contents

Acknowledgements

This book is the result of many years' interest in AEC vehicles. My information has been gathered from many sources and I would like to thank the many people who are too numerous to mention individually — fellow Society members, staff of operators and manufacturers as well as former colleagues at Southall and the former depots at West Bromwich and St Helens.

The Omnibus Society and the PSV Circle through their meetings, visits to operators and publications which are compiled from the recording of vehicles through out the country and abroad, have given me considerable help with vehicle details. I very much appreciate their permission to use information obtained from their fleet histories, etc. I also feel that a great debt is owed to the Historic Commercial Vehicle Club and the more recently formed societies for fostering vehicle preservation enabling many interesting vehicles to be saved or rescued from the scrap heap. This gives ours and future generations a glimpse of the past with the products from Southall being in the forefront.

The selection of photographs has been most difficult to make and many interesting ones have had to be left out. My thanks go to the many photographers whose views I have used and also to those whose work has been left out — it is to be hoped that there will be another time as there are many facets not covered here. Again Ron Rushton has aided my task by copying and printing many of the illustrations used. Some superb prints have been obtained from glass plates of varying quality. The help of John Senior of the Transport Publishing Company in making these available to me has enabled several gaps in the story to be filled. Chris Taylor also widened the scope by supplying a large number of photographs and details of vehicles of the 1920s and 1930s — periods that were not covered very well photographically.

I am very grateful to Gerry Truran and Harry Pick for the time spent in reading through my draft manuscript and for their helpful comments and additional information.

Below: Following two Walsall 663T chassis in 1931 were 60 for London United Tramways with UCC bodies (both companies being LGOC subsidiaries) seating 56. Nicknamed 'diddlers' because of their half cab layout, but they were not as confusing as the Notts and Derby buses delivered in the following years 1932-3. They gave between 15 and 20 years' service. N. J. Treacher Collection

Introduction

Although the production lines ran for the last time at the end of May 1979, 18 months later it is still hard to believe that the AEC marque has ended. Admittedly it was many months afterwards before the last Reliances left the factory and entered service. The letters AEC meant a lot to operators and enthusiasts alike. The AEC vehicles weren't perfect — neither were their competitors — but they were reliable, had a good performance and gave the passengers an enjoyable and musical ride. Although it was a large company its personnel cared, creating a good customer relationship and loyalty. Some customers have transferred their allegiance to the other Leyland group products but others, when they could no longer buy AECs bought from competitors, many moving to foreign chassis.

Production of buses began in 1910 at the former Vanguard garage at Walthamstow and output grew steadily until the premises were not large enough, resulting in a new factory being built at Southall. A link however with this birthplace was maintained until the end in 1979 by the retention of the original telegraphic address — Vangastow.

The new purpose-built factory was completed in 1926 and production was transferred to the 63-acre site. It was a triangular shaped piece of land (inspiration for the famous trademark?) bounded by the Grand Union Canal on one side, the main railway line from London to the West Country on another with the third boundary being Windmill Lane which led to the Uxbridge road, over which was the Iron Bridge carrying the railway and an advert for AEC.

Nearby was the London Transport Hanwell (now Southall) garage. Most official photographs were taken on the main drive alongside the railway line and the growth of the row of poplars lining the drive can be seen over the years.

The original purpose of the Associated Equipment Company Ltd was to build buses but it was also responsible for supplies needed to run the horse buses. An agreement was reached in 1913 with Daimler for that company to sell surplus production to outside customers. This agreement lasted until 1916 when the War Office had more pressing demands. The link was reformed a decade later with the formation of the Associated Daimler Co Ltd. Both companies co-operated in the design of chassis which were fitted with engines from both firms. The agreement lasted for about two years before they went their separate ways again.

Whilst AEC's main concern was to fulfil the needs of the London General Omnibus Company for buses, chassis were also sold to outside concerns. Lorry chassis became part of the production at Southall as well as overseas business from the early 1920s. When the London Passenger Transport Board was formed in 1933, there was an agreement for AEC to supply 90% of its bus requirements for ten years, and this was subsequently renewed for another five years. When that expired, AEC was very glad that Leyland had secured orders for the 500 RTWs and over 1,600 RTLs as it was having difficulty in meeting a considerable number of orders for its products from all over the world.

In 1948, due to Government nationalisation policies, it seemed that there would be a big reduction

Below: *The 'new' factory was situated on a 63 acre, triangular site off Windmill Lane at Southall. After its sale in 1980, the majority of the buildings were demolished and new ones erected in their place for smaller firms.* AEC Ltd

in demand for buses and lorries at home. With a view to consolidating its position, Crossley Motors Ltd of Stockport and the Maudslay Motor Company Ltd of Alcester were purchased, leading to the formation of Associated Commercial Vehicles Ltd. Both the acquired companies were bus chassis manufacturers, with Maudslay also producing trucks and Crossley bus bodywork and trolleybuses. Their range of chassis were superseded by AEC designs — the last Maudslays entering service in 1950 and Crossleys in 1952. The latter continued to build bus bodywork and indeed built the last BUT trolleybus chassis. Maudslay however built some Regal Mk IV chassis and nine Regent Mk IIIs in 1951 plus short wheelbase Regent Mk III chassis for Merryweather who used them as the basis of their fire appliances. The factory later turned over to producing axles for Southall and was sold to the American Rockwell Group who continued to supply units for Leyland chassis.

In 1949 the group expanded still further with the purchase of Park Royal Vehicles Ltd, and their subsidiary Charles H. Roe Ltd, of Leeds — both bodybuilders.

In the 1950s the export business was developed extensively with assembly, and in some cases manufacture, in various countries including the Netherlands, Belgium, Portugal, Spain, France, South Africa and Argentina. In South America since the 1920s, AEC buses were sold as ACLO, due to objections by the German firm of AEG who thought there would be confusion of the similar initials.

In 1961 Transport Equipment (Thornycroft) Ltd, with a factory at Basingstoke was acquired. Its products ranged from 5-6ton models up to the very large vehicles for export such as the Mighty Antar which was also used by the British Army. Whilst AEC looked at the possibility of continuing the home market models, they were expensive to product and the increasing competition from mass production manufacturers making vehicles for bigger payloads made it uneconomic. Some export chassis were retained and production of the AEC Dumptruck plus gearboxes was transferred to Basingstoke. Vehicle production ceased when the Dumptruck was transferred to Scammell, the factory then producing solely gearboxes. It was sold to the gearbox manufacturing group — Eaton — who still supply these AEC-designed gearboxes to Leyland Vehicles.

In 1962, an even bigger link up occurred with AEC's main rival — Leyland. This made economic sense in the overseas business by co-operating instead of competing. Leyland and AEC each had its overseas distributors.

In some countries they both sold large numbers, in others one was more popular than the other. One area where Leyland dominated was Israel whilst in the Arab countries AEC was supreme. After the linking great pains were taken for many years not to make this public knowledge in those countries because of their antagonism for each other.

It was also Leyland's policy to sell all vehicles overseas as Leylands and this continued after BMC was acquired in 1968, adding Guy and Daimler to the fold in Britain, but as additional Leyland models overseas. All new designs in this country also carried the Leyland badge. Consequently the AEC letters were

Left: *The last building to be opened on the 63 acre Southall site was this one for the chassis despatch dept. Built in 1961, the testing, final inspection and preparing the chassis for delivery were all carried out here. This view shows some of the variety made at that time. In the foreground is a Regent 5 double-decker chassis alongside a Mercury 16 tons gross goods vehicle. In the central line are some AEC Reliance chassis, whilst the models against the wall are mainly export bonneted Mogul chassis, two Military Militants and two Routemaster buses.* AEC Ltd

Below: *Maudslay's postwar PSV production was of the Marathon — a maximum length single-decker. It was unique in offering a petrol engine but this Whitson-bodied coach was on the Mk 3 version powered by an AEC 7.7 litre oil engine.* N. J. Treacher

borne by fewer and fewer vehicles leaving Southall and towards the end even the Reliance was sold as Leyland. However, on some of the last to be built, due to a change in specification on the front axle to give an improved brake lining life, AEC axles were fitted in place of the rationalised group design, resulting in AEC badges being fitted to the hub caps again.

After the closure of Southall in May 1979, many chassis were unfinished and completion of these took several months. The offices had been left as though the staff were to return, with pencils, notebooks, etc, on the desks. Early in 1980 the machinery was sold and the premises bought by a property company for redevelopment with the buildings being demolished. It is interesting to record that the last person to leave the premises on the day of transfer 11 July 1980 was Mr Harry Pick, Oldbury Depot Manager for Leyland Vehicles Ltd, who had started work with AEC about 40 years previously.

So ended an era. With the introduction of the Bus Grant Scheme in the 1960s which favoured one-man operation, sales of AEC double-deckers ceased as they had not developed a suitable design. If the rear engined FRM had entered production it may have been a different story. On the single-deck model, the rear-engined Swift which had sold well was discontinued in favour of the Leyland National in the early 1970s and sales of the Reliance to NBC companies were largely dropped in favour of the Leopard.

Independents continued to buy the Reliance with sales of about 100 a year towards the end. The number of Regents in service is rapidly dwindling and the Reliance is disappearing from major fleets. AECs had a character of their own with pleasant sounding engines coupled to 'musical' gearboxes. Their passing is regretted by many people. Fortunately there are a large number of preserved examples around to bear lasting tribute.

Above: Crossley's postwar output was mainly double-deck chassis, many of which were bodied in its own bodyshop, which continued in production after chassis manufacture ceased in 1952. This is an all Crossley bus for its local corporation — Stockport — built in 1949.
N. J. Treacher Collection

Above right: Park Royal joined forces with ACV in 1949. At that time its main output was of double-deck bodies and it had an agreement to supply metal frameworks to Guy Motors. This is a bus completed in 1952 for one of the three Doncaster independents which were Guy customers for two decades after having their first Arabs allocated to them during the war. It was withdrawn in 1969.
R. N. Hannay

Right: As a subsidiary of Park Royal, Charles H. Roe joined the ACV group. Its products had two outstanding features for many years — a robust framework constructed of teak, and a metal waist rail which made identification of the body easy but had a practical advantage of protecting the body from side damage. This is a 55-seat lowbridge body built in 1950 and mounted on a reconditioned 1938 Bristol K5G chassis which is now preserved.
R. N. Hannay

Within the constraints of this book, it is only possible to give a brief look at the wide range of passenger vehicles that came from AEC, and their users. The history is very closely tied to London General and its successors. Space has only allowed a few photographs of London buses to be included. I do not intend this to be a slur on the importance of developments in the Capital city but feel that there are many excellent books produced by Ian Allan Ltd and other publishers that cover this side of the history in great detail. I do hope that you will find this book interesting and informative and forgive this omission to the record of a firm whose slogan for many years was — 'Builders of London's buses'.

Goostrey, Cheshire   *Robin Hannay*
January 1981

11

Above: *When Transport Equipment (Thornycroft) Ltd was acquired in 1961, no passenger vehicles had been built for the home market for many years. One of their earlier products — a 1919 model J with 34-seat ex-LGOC body by Dodson has been preserved by Portsmouth Corporation after being withdrawn in 1927.*
N. J. Treacher

1 The Formation of AEC

The origins of the AEC company can be traced back to 1820 with the beginning of horse bus operation in Paris which were merged into one company in 1854. In the following year, the directors decided to form a company to acquire services in London. It was registered as the Compagnie Générale des Omnibus de Londres having a capital of £1million and the registered office in Paris. Services were run with horse buses, an increasing number being double-deck.

The services of other operators were acquired, the largest being the London Motor Bus Company (Vanguard) in July 1908. Vanguard's fleet included almost 400 motor buses, and these joined a slightly larger number operated by the London General Omnibus Company (as the French company had been renamed). After an assessment of the multitude of types owned, the LGOC decided to build a model of its own, in the former Vanguard Works at Walthamstow. The prototype entered service in December 1909 and

was followed by 60 more in the following six months. Known as the X type, it had normal control and used a four-cylinder, 28hp petrol engine, a gearbox using chains and sprockets for quietness.

Experience gained from the X resulted in an improved chassis — the B type. Initially using the same engine as the X, the bore and stroke were subsequently increased to give ultimately 45bhp. The

Below: *United Automobile Services in its early days covered a very large territory from East Anglia to Northumberland. Prior to its split in 1931, AEC was the major purchase. This is an early example of a Y type, possibly ex-WD with one of their own bus bodies, built in 1919. An advertisement board on the roof at the front reads: 'Shop at Binns' — still a current exhortation 60 years later. An advert for one of the early suppliers of petrol — Pratts — is attached to the top of the radiator.* C. Taylor

speed limit of 12mph was achieved at 750rpm, but as the engine could run up to 2,000rpm (a high figure in those days) speeds of over 30mph could be obtained.

With the increase in chassis production, a separate company was formed in July 1912 by the LGOC for this purpose. At the same time LGOC acquired the Metropolitan Electric Tramways Group which had recently ordered a large number of Daimler buses with an agreement for them to be maintained by the Daimler company. As a result, reorganisation took place resulting in a decrease in the number of Daimler chassis on order and the discontinuation of the maintenance contract. As compensation LGOC allowed Daimler to sell surplus AEC production — the only difference being the radiator, although a Daimler 5.7litre, sleeve valve engine was fitted in the CC model. This arrangement was dissolved in the middle of 1916 when the Government assumed control of production for the duration of the war. One result was the fitment of the 45bhp Tylor engine to enable some standardisation of components of vehicles in military service. Chassis so equipped were redesignated the Y type 3/4-tonners and until the split carried 'Daimler' on the radiator. This model made up 40% of the vehicles supplied to the forces and over 10,000 were built. One interesting feature was the installation of a moving track to speed production — probably the first in the world for commercial vehicles — and a completed chassis came off the line every 30 minutes.

Many B types were commandeered at the beginning of World War 1. Over 1,300 went to France with a further 300 engaged on military service in the London area. One of the buses that saw action in France (B340) became one of the first buses to be preserved in this country when withdrawn in December 1924. It was then overhauled at Chiswick and repainted but stored under dust sheets. In 1936 it was shipped to Canada for Golden Jubilee celebrations for nine months. It is now at the London Transport museum in Covent Garden.

With the end of the war, thoughts were turned to new vehicles. Emerging in August 1919, the new 300 series model, the K type, had a 28hp engine, which by virtue of having all the auxiliaries (carburettor, magneto, plugs etc) on the nearside, enabled the driver to be placed further forwards. This allowed more body space and as the chassis was lighter than the B, another 12 passengers could be carried within a gross weight of 7ton. This model also introduced purpose-built bodies for motor bus work, and by incorporating wheel arches, a lower floor level was achieved and the full width of the lower saloon had

Below: The police constable was assisting the photographer in obtaining this view of a party setting out in a solid tyred Y type chassis with a 27-seat charabanc body in 1920. AEC Ltd

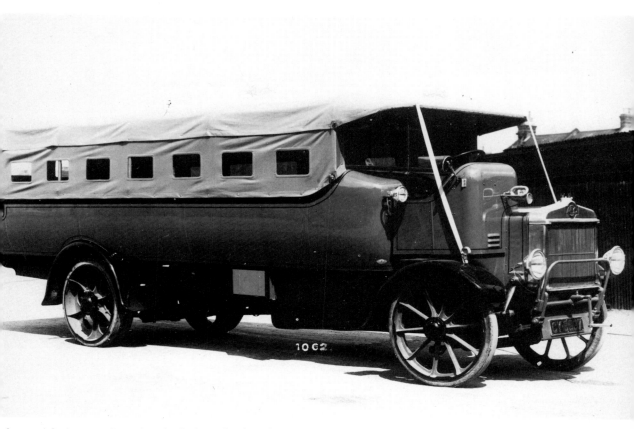

Above: *Three of the 29 model 503 chassis bought by South Wales Transport in 1924, received archaic looking Strachan & Brown 32-seat all-weather coach bodies like this one, which when sold, became a lorry in the Cardiff area; it was withdrawn in 1938.* Author's Collection

forward-facing seating ahead of the wheel arches. Main production ended in 1921 by which time London had 1,060 in use but further batches between 1924 and 1926 increased the total to 1,132 plus 24 single-deckers.

A further increase in the gross vehicle weight — to 8.5ton — enabled more passengers to be carried. The S type entered service in January 1921 seating 54 in an overall length of 24ft 8in. The driver was moved fully alongside the engine which was rated at 35hp. When sold to provincial operators the bus was designated the 403 type and a 45hp option was available from 1922. AEC also made some of its own (Burt) sleeve valve engines and these experimental units went in to LGOC 406 series chassis. Having achieved a high carrying capacity, the LGOC engineers turned their thoughts to improving the design. The result appeared in 1923 as a closed-top NS-type. The centre of gravity was lowered by using for the first time, a pressed steel frame, which was downswept behind the engine and lower still after the rear axle to give a low platform height, compared with a step up to the platform on previous buses. However, the Metropolitan Police considered the roof would make the bus top-heavy and would not allow them to be fitted until October 1925 when four entered service experimentally. These were subsequently approved and in 1928 pneumatic tyres were able to be fitted

when the overall width limit was increased to 7ft 5in. Known as the NS, most members of the class subsequently received both improvements, but chassis sold to other operators had these features much earlier. Single-deck bodies were also fitted and many were exported.

The largest engine fitted so far was the 45hp Tylor used in the Y type chassis. When the S type range started in 1923, a bigger AEC engine powered the S type with a capacity of 6.8litre. Models 501 and 505 used Y type chassis but the 502/3/4 were based on S types. Normal or forward control could be provided. When the 507 model for double-deck bodywork was introduced, it as well received a type name — Ramilies. As was common at this time, all types of chassis were also sold as trucks. A normal control version was given the type number 506 and 508 were forward control goods vehicles, with 507 and 509. Production continued of this series until 1930 with the last 506 being built in 1932.

Above: *Belfast Corporation's first buses were six model 413s with 30-seat rear entrance bodies by Short. New in 1926, they were withdrawn in 1934 and scrapped.*
W. Montgomery

Left: *The bulk of South Wales Transport's purchases in 1924 were the more powerful provincial version of the S — the 503. Most received 54 seat open-top bodies, this being one of 15 built by Ransomes. Withdrawn in 1932, no further user has been found.*
C. Taylor

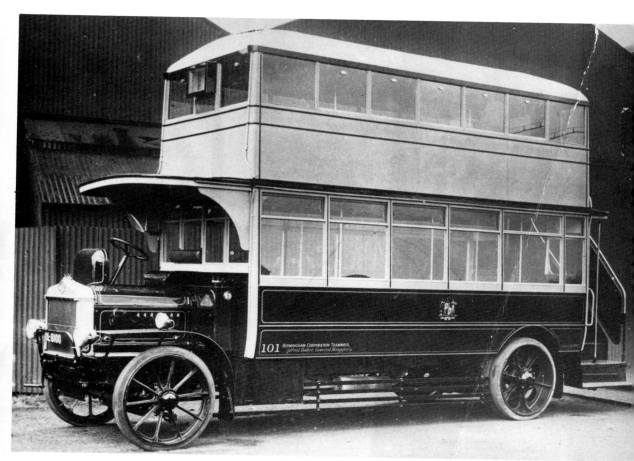

Top: *Whilst covered top double-deckers were not allowed in London until 1926, Birmingham put this 504 with a 50-seat Brush body on the road in 1924. In the next two years a further 105 were bought with bodies from three different builders.*   B. W. Baker Collection

Above: *This pair of 505 model chassis were new in 1925 with Strachan and Brown 32-seat bodies. They had been withdrawn by the time the Lanarkshire company was acquired by Central SMT in August 1932. It remained as a separate fleet until November 1949.*   Author's Collection

Above: The AEC 2 series were usually 2 ton payload lorries but a few received bus bodies. This 24-seat 202 model has LGOC bodywork and was built for its subsidiary in 1925 and was returned in 1930.   H. J. Snook

Left: This is a 411 model fitted with a single-deck body, believed built by United Automobile Services, which has an unusual rear entrance. Ralphs Garages became a subsidiary of Red and White.   C. Taylor

Below left: The replacement for the Y type was the 506. This was one of six built in 1926 for Devon General with 32-seat bodies by Hall Lewis. They were joined by 12 similar ADC models in the following year.   C. Taylor

Above right: The large normal-control bus chassis sold in limited numbers in this country, and AEC versions are even rarer. In 1926, Strachan and Brown built this 26-seat body on a 414 chassis for a Cambridgeshire independent who ran it for six years. Author's Collection

Right: The provincial version of the NS was the 409. Ten closed-top 52-seaters complete with LGOC bodywork were bought by the Waterloo and Crosby Motor Services in 1926. When the firm was acquired by Ribble in 1930, it ran them for another two years. J. F. Higham

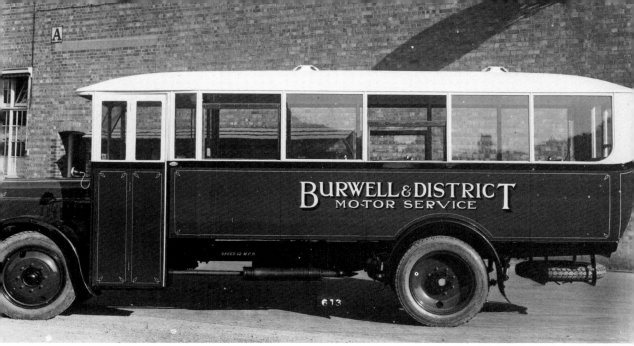

Left: *The first motorbuses operated by Bradford City Tramways were 10 model 413s with 28-seat bodies by United Automobile Services, delivered in 1926. They gave between five and nine years service.* Ian Allan Library

Below: *Greyhound Motors Ltd, of Bristol was formed in 1921 to take over two long-established businesses. Local services were run in competition with Bristol Tramways, as well as long distance routes. Their service to London started in February 1925 became the longest distance express route operating all the year round. Bristol Tramways acquired the company in March 1928 and absorbed the vehicles into its own fleet on 1 January 1936. Amongst the 77 vehicles transferred were five of these 409s with LGOC 52-seat bodies bought in 1926 with covered top decks — a feature that was only allowed in London later in the year. Pneumatic tyres were subsequently fitted and the buses were withdrawn during 1936.* AEC Ltd

2 Associated Daimlers

Another link with Daimler was forged in June 1926 when Associated Daimler Co Ltd, was formed to sell both AEC and Daimler products. The AEC 4 and 5 chassis were used fitted with engines from both factories, with a new radiator which carried the name AssociateD DaimleR on the top tank. AEC's power unit was a 5.1litre four-cylinder engine developing 45bhp at 1,000rpm, whereas the Daimler engine was a faster revving 3.568litre six-cylinder producing 70bhp at 3,000rpm. The latter also had sleeve valves making it quiet in operation. Chassis designations had letter A or D as a suffix to indicate the make of engine powering it. Most were forward control models but over 100 normal control chassis were sold.

The model range started with the 413, 14ft 6in wheelbase chassis with a straight frame for about 30-seat bodies. This was originally introduced in 1923 as model 411, and was the first AEC type to be named as well, being called the Renown. It was also AEC's first chassis on pneumatic tyres. In 1924 the specification was improved by having hand and foot brakes operating in the rear brake drums, instead of separately; this improved version was renumbered 413 and a longer wheelbase version was designated the 415. The 416 took the design further ahead by using a dropped chassis frame and was the first true ADC model, with a normal control version the 417. These models also had the option of front wheel brakes if required plus vacuum servo assistance as a further refinement. Produced until 1929, about 1,000 416s were sold. Model 418 was a lorry chassis but the 419 was a special normal control model with a sheet metal radiator shell and the Daimler six-cylinder engine built for the LGOC.

Production was moved in 1926 to a new factory at Southall. From here came some double-deckers — the NS now titled 422, and available with pneumatic tyres for both London General and other operators built until 1929.

Below: *The Belfast Omnibus Company was the largest constituent of the Northern Ireland Road Transport Board in 1935. The fleet of about 170 was almost wholly on ADC or chassis. In 1927/8, 98 ADC model 416 chassis, mainly with Hall Lewis or Dodson 32-seat bodies, were bought. Five buses are seen here on delivery, the last two having the older radiator with the cast name. They were withdrawn in 1936.* Author's Collection

The year 1926 also saw a great interest in six-wheeled buses, with Guy leading the way. This spurred the LGOC to design a competitor, which entered service in 1927 as the model 802; this had the six-cylinder 5.7 litre Daimler sleeve valve engine which was also used by Guy! The 802 had a forward control layout and a remotely mounted four-speed gearbox. The LGOC built a 68-seat body on it and numbered the resulting vehicle LS1. Two further chassis proved useful at AEC in accommodating 104 passengers in a similar body by using gangway seats. These were used to convey work-people who lived in the Walthamstow area to the new factory at Southall. Claimed to be the world's largest capacity bus, it was used as an experimental vehicle and had the prototype AEC oil engine installed at the end of 1928, making it the first with this type of power unit in this country, if not in the world. LGOC had 12 802 chassis altogether — one receiving a single-deck body, and five demonstrators were built, but were not very successful.

Towards the end of 1927, the Daimler works in Coventry began building chassis similar to the model 416, powered by a Daimler engine and having a different radiator with a plain top tank. Model number 423 was allocated to the design or 424 if it had normal control. These were followed by the 425 and 426 — similar models built at Southall with AEC engines. These models heralded the dissolution of the ADC, which occurred in July 1928.

Below: *Autocar Services of Tunbridge Wells was acquired by East Surrey Traction in 1928. When the latter's services were integrated in the LPTB in 1933, Autocar Services was transferred to Maidstone and District in July 1933. The 82-bus fleet ranged in age from two to nine years old — all but one being from ADC or AEC. These are four of five 416s bought in 1927 with 32-seat Hall Lewis bodies. They were amongst 25 buses sold in 1935 to AEC which acted as dealer, in part exchange for new Regents.* Author's Collection

Right: *This is an extremely interesting photograph of a 416 when new in 1927 for Samuel Johnson's Supreme fleet, from Stourbridge, Worcestershire. The body has a folding canvas hood and full drop windows to enable passengers to take full advantage of good weather. A similar chassis was restored in 1981 and fitted with a replica body by Wyatts of Tean, Staffordshire, which made a superb job of it, as they did on several other similar projects.* C. Taylor Collection

Below right: *Eastern Express Motors Ltd was formed in 1927 and acquired by United Automobile Services in January 1930. This 416 with Strachan & Brown 32-seat bodywork was one of 12 bought in 1928, eight of which went to United and three to Northern General. This bus was sold by United in 1934, going to a Welsh operator which was acquired by Red and White in 1936 with the bus running to the end of 1937.* Author's Collection

23

Top: *Samuelson's Saloon Coaches started a London to Birmingham via Oxford service in January 1928 and later a Liverpool service running via Dunstable, Birmingham and Chester, the route being shown schematically on roof boards. This is one of a pair of 28-seater Phoenix-bodied ADC 426s delivered in October 1928 for the new service. They had the improved radiator and dumb iron covers introduced earlier in the year. This company was sold to Red and White in 1931. An associated company, Samuelsons New Transport Co Ltd, existed until the 1970s.* Author's Collection

Above: *Although Timpsons headquarters was at Catford in south-east London, they had thriving businesses in Torquay and Hastings. In 1932 the Torquay operations were sold to Devon General and two years later Maidstone & District took over the fleet of 67 vehicles in Hastings. This ADC 417, new in 1928, although registered in that town was not amongst the vehicles acquired. It is seen leaving Catford for Great Yarmouth. Hall Lewis built the 25-seat body. The passengers' luggage was carried on a rack mounted on the solid roof section and enclosed by a tarpaulin cover.* N. J. Treacher Collection

3 The Three Rs: Rackham, Reliance and Regent

AEC

The AEC range was powered by four-cylinder engines whilst its competitors were introducing six-cylinder power units giving a livelier and smoother performance which was being called for by the rapidly expanding coach industry. Work on rectifying this deficiency was started in 1928 by a new chief engineer — G. J. Rackham who rejoined the company after a gap of 12 years. During this period he had been involved in the early tanks and then went to America where he became the chief engineer of Yellow Coach in 1922. Returning to the UK four years later, he joined Leyland in a similar position. There he developed a new range of improved passenger chassis powered by six-cylinder engines — the Tiger and the Titan.

Within a short time of taking office at Southall Rackham put a six-cylinder, 6.1litre engine in the Reliance chassis, the designation being changed from 426 to 660. The radiator, which had previously lacked

the company's logo, had an inverted triangle added with about two thirds of it projecting below the top tank — this trade mark lasted for over half a century. At the top of the triangle was a representation of the London General bullseye with the letters AEC on the bar. The chassis retained a cone clutch and four-speed gearbox. Although the 660 Reliance was only an

Below: *G. J. Rackham's first project was to design a six-cylinder engine which went into a single-deck chassis. Named the Reliance this chassis was one of a batch of 43 bought by A. Timpson & Co Ltd, of London. New in May 1929 it was allocated originally to its Grey Cars subsidiary fleet in Torquay. After acquisition by Maidstone and District, the original Hall Lewis 30-seat body was replaced (along with 25 others) in 1936 by a Harrington 32-seat coach body. In 1949 the chassis was scrapped but the body was transferred to a Regal Mk III.* Author's Collection

interim product, it continued for four years and a total of almost 500 was built. The next model — the 661 — emerged early in 1929 bearing the name Regent. This double-decker chassis was a completely new model using only the six-cylinder power unit of the Reliance; a single-plate clutch eased the driver's effort and allowed the power to be transmitted to a unit-mounted four-speed gearbox. The drive line was down the nearside of the chassis to an underslung worm rear axle of the semi-floating type. The Regent was designed with a 15ft 6.5in wheelbase for the maximum legal length of 25ft, but in 1930 this was increased to 26ft with a 16ft 3in wheelbase — a dimension which remained constant until there was a further increase of one foot in the overall length in 1950. Many components of the original Regent were still being used at that time. Mechanical developments continued with a larger 7.4litre six-cylinder engine in 1931 and a fully floating rear axle in 1932.

One feature that has only been mentioned briefly so far, is the oil engine. AEC was in the forefront of development of this form of power unit in this country. Its first was installed in the six-wheeled works bus of 1928, another one emerged in 1930 which bore no resemblance to the original prototype. This was an 8.1litre 95bhp indirect injection type which was fitted into a demonstration Regent double-decker, with three similar engines going into London General ST buses, and nine later going into LT buses. Operational trials were also conducted with oil-engined Regents in Walsall, Birmingham, Glasgow and Halifax corporations' fleets and also with company operators. From the results of the trials, it was decided a more power-

ful engine was desirable and an 8.8litre unit came in 1931. This was originally governed at a high speed even for large petrol engines — 2,400rpm — but later this figure was reduced to 2,200rpm at which speed 130bhp was produced. An increasing number of customers opted for the oil engine particularly London General and subsequently London Transport.

To digress slightly, the formation of the London Passenger Transport Board on 1 July 1933 led to the Associated Equipment Co Ltd becoming a separate entity. Direct control of the company by London General ceased, but an agreement was made by which AEC was to supply at least 90% of London General's requirements. This gave AEC a firm foundation on

Below: The Great Northern Railway (Ireland) Ltd, started operating buses in 1928 and by acquisition of businesses on both sides of the border built up a large fleet. A portion of the fleet (50 buses) became part of the NIRTB on its formation in 1935 and 77 buses went to CIE in 1959. Thirty years earlier 20 Reliances were purchased; fourteen chassis received new bodies built by the GNR workshops between 1931 and 1936 — the other buses were sold in the following year. The remaining buses were withdrawn between 1940 and 1949. AEC Ltd

Right: The ninth Regent chassis was bought by Wallasey Corporation in July 1929. The body, built by Short seated 24 in each saloon. Upstairs the seats were fitted in the centre with gangways on both sides. A hump in the roof gave good headroom, and the arrangement allowed the buses to go under lower bridges than those with the conventional arrangement having a centre gangway. This was a common feature of the period.
N. J. Treacher Collection

Left: *Thomas Tilling operated buses in London as well as Brighton in the early 1930s. They ordered 296 Regents between 1930 and 1932, the first 12 coming to the Brighton branch later Brighton, Hove and District. The Tilling-built body was later modified by ECW to enable the top to be removed. Sold in 1950, it went to Crosville who withdrew it in 1954. The original petrol engine had been replaced by a 7.7litre oil engine in 1946.* N. J. Treacher

Below: *Borough Services Ltd, which was based in Southend-on-Sea, was acquired by Eastern National in 1933 but ran as a separate company until 1940. Amongst the 18 buses taken over were six Regents, two of which had only just entered service. This bus, JN 343, was one of three bought in 1930 and had a 50-seat Park Royal body. It was withdrawn in 1936 and surprisingly disappeared without trace, whilst one of its sisters ran for another 20 years with Eastern National.* Author's Collection

which to base its new-found independence, but was not a complete necessity — AEC's passenger vehicle business had been built up at home and abroad and sales of goods vehicles were already substantial.

Returning to PSV developments, as many municipalities and a few companies were replacing tramway systems, they wanted simpler buses to drive. Daimler had a preselector gearbox based on Wilson patents which was a step in the right direction. Apart from making gear changing simpler, the fluid flywheel helped to reduce transmission shocks. London General bought three Daimler CH6 chassis and these entered service in 1931. Subsequently three sets of gearboxes and fluid flywheels were fitted into two LT and one ST chassis and later more sets were purchased for fitment into buses for London General and other operators. In 1934 AEC obtained permission to manufacture the transmission under licence and in the late 1940s supplied it to Leyland for the RTL and RTW chassis plus some PD2s for Leeds. Instead of the Daimler system using a quadrant mounted on the steering column, AEC had a floor-mounted gear lever to change the gears, with a smaller knob than the 'crash' box gear lever.

The Regent had an alternative oil engine fitted into 11 chassis for London General in 1933. This was a more compact unit developed for use in the Q type bus with a swept volume of 7.74litre, having a bore of 106mm with a stroke of 146mm. In 1935, the bore was reduced by 1mm, giving a capacity of 7,585cc

but the name '7.7' stuck and, in fact, was used incorrectly by many people when speaking about the 470 engine of the 1950s. In 1936 the original indirect combustion system designed by Ricardo, was changed to direct injection. While efficiency was improved, this had the effect of lowering the power output to 90bhp, although the maximum revs were only 1,750 — the previous engine was governed at 2,000rpm at which speed 115bhp was produced. This engine was to remain in production until 1953 but revs were increased slightly to 1,800, giving 98bhp.

Gradually the 8.8litre engine gave way to the smaller 7.7. However, some customers called for the 102bhp Gardner 6LW, chassis going to Aberdeen, Dundee and Huddersfield with Kingston-upon-Hull taking 85bhp 5LWs in 1939.

London Transport, naturally, was the largest customer for the Regent. Taking into account acquired buses, the ST class totalled 1,139 with the number of the STL (ST-long), based on the longer 16ft 3in wheelbase chassis, reaching 2,625 in 1939. Early customers for the Regent also included Wallasey, Birmingham, Nottingham, Halifax, Newcastle, Sheffield, Chester and Glasgow corporations. Apart

Below: One of the first oil-engined Regents was purchased by Western National, being delivered in 1931 with a 48-seat lowbridge body by Short. The unusual and ugly treatment of the front should be noted. Rebodied by Beadle in 1945, it was withdrawn 10 years later. Author's Collection

Above: *Originally carrying a Brush 56-seat highbridge body when new in 1932 this Western National Regent was given a new lease of life when it was rebodied by Beadle in 1942 with the 52-seat body shown. The petrol engine was replaced by a Gardner 5LW oil engine in 1938. When withdrawn in 1954 the bus was purchased by a showman.* A. R. Packer

Below: *Six of the 20 double-deckers bought by Salford in 1934 were oil-engined Regents. This is the first of the batch which had MCCW 48-seat bodies. They were withdrawn between 1949 and 1951. AECs continued to be ordered each year up to 1940, with one batch in postwar years.* AEC Ltd

from LGOC associated companies, National Omnibus and Transport Co Ltd, and two export chassis, over 100 were sold before the first company order was placed by City of Oxford for 18, which entered service in 1930. Another 400 chassis went to LGOC and small fleets before another major company order was placed — by National — for nine, seven of which went to the Eastern fleet and two to the Southern, and a large repeat order for 77 was placed by Birmingham. The list of new customers grew and several demonstrators were built to enable operators to register and run them for a while before deciding whether to purchase.

The oil engine began to be fitted late in 1930 with LGOC ST 462 being the first followed by ST 464 and 466. The next engines were for buses destined for Glasgow, Walsall, Halifax and Birmingham corporations in 1930 and the first for an English company was delivered to Western National in 1931. It is interesting to note that due to the extra weight of the engine and heavier batteries to start it, the seating capacity was reduced from 51 for the petrol-engined buses in the same batch to 48. The LGOC had meanwhile had nine LT type AEC Renowns with A155 8.1litre engines and turned to the A161 8.85litre when that became available. Following quickly on the Western National Regent were examples for Leicester and Stockton with Lowestoft, Wallasey, Portsmouth and Dundee corporations taking delivery later in the year. In 1932 three demonstrators were built and were purchased by Sheffield, Cardiff and Bradford corporations. Surprisingly the second oil-engined double-deck bus for a company was not built until 1933 when one was purchased by a Scottish independent — Baillie Bros of Dumbarton — fitted with a 52-seat Roe lowbridge body. The first customer to accept the oil engine as standard was Halifax corporation in 1933. In the same year 11 STLs entered service with oil engines and this became the standard power unit in the following year.

Engines were supplied to convert operators' vehicles, including some to Midland Red and Bristol, and as a consequence of this and comparable endeavours by rival engine manufacturers the operators began to standardise on the oil engine. Whilst the 8.8litre engine was the first production model and it continued to be available to the outbreak of war, the majority of chassis received the 7.7litre (and subsequently 7.58litre) power units. When production ceased after the outbreak of war well over 7,000 Regents had been sold. In 1941 a further 92 chassis were built from parts available to ease the shortage of buses. These were allocated to a large number of operators and had the direct injection 7.7litre engine and four-speed 'crash' gearbox.

A normal control version of the Regent chassis was sold as a goods vehicle, called the Mandator. The model number was 672, and one of these which started life as a fuel tanker was acquired by Gosport & Fareham Omnibus Company in 1944, and rebodied as a double-decker.

Right: *Great Yarmouth bought seven oil-engined Regents in 1934. The bodies were built by English Electric and had 48 seats. Loaned to Coventry Corporation from 1940 to 1945, this bus went for scrap when withdrawn in 1960.   AEC Ltd*

Below: *Some operators in the 1930s favoured forward entrance double-deck bodies. This is one of 30 bought by Trent in 1937 with 56-seat Weymann bodywork. They had 7.7 litre engines and preselector gearboxes. In 1949 this bus was one of several rebodied by Willowbrook with a 55-seat lowbridge body. Withdrawn in 1960, it went to Howells & Withers of Pontllanfraith who sold it in the following year.*
Roy Marshall Collection

Above: *Having a pleasant and sunny climate, Eastbourne has run open-top double-deckers for many years. This petrol-engined Regent with NCME 48-seat body was one of five bought in 1938. It was converted to open-top in 1954 and four extra seats added to the upper deck. It was fitted with a Leyland 8.6litre oil engine in the same year. Withdrawn in 1962, it went for scrap.*
N. J. Treacher

Left: *In 1938, Glasgow Corporation put 85 Regents into service with appropriate registrations — BUS 101-85. This is one of 60 bodied by Weymann as a 56-seater. Withdrawn in 1951 it went to Miller of Cirencester before being sold in 1955 to Gosport and Fareham. Unfortunately it was one of the buses destroyed in a fire in 1957.*
N. J. Treacher Collection

Below left: *Barton Transport's first new AEC double-deckers were two unfrozen Regents allocated in 1942 with 55-seat lowbridge bodies by NCB (Northern Coachbuilders). These were bought by Campbell of Pitsea, Essex in 1948. This bus was sold early in 1956 but its sister ran for a few months longer after the business was acquired by Eastern National later in the year.*
N. J. Treacher

4 Early Regals

The previous chapter covered the development of the Regent chassis by G. J. Rackham and the introduction prior to this of the six-cylinder engine. The single-deck version of the Regent was called the Regal model 662. Legal overall length was then limited to 26ft and a 17ft wheelbase was used. The six-cylinder 6.1litre engine of the Reliance was retained but a single-plate clutch transmitted the power to four-speed gearbox bolted directly to the engine. A new rear axle was adopted of the semi-floating type. This was subsequently replaced by a fully floating design in 1932.

As with the Regent, the oil engined Regal became available and an early customer was Scottish Motor Traction (now Eastern Scottish). Midland Bus, an SMT associate bought three Wycombe-bodied examples for use on its Glasgow-London route, accumulating a high mileage in a comparatively short time. London General had three Ts with 8.1litre oil engines in 1930, but these were subsequently replaced by 8.8litre versions, and one chassis received an eight-cylinder petrol engine. The wheelbase of the latter was reduced by 6in to achieve the correct weight distribution. It was not until 1936 that the oil engine was standardised for London Transport single-deckers with a batch of 100 with 7.7 engines which became 9T9 Green Line coaches, while, in 1938-9 226 were received with 8.8litre engines which formed the 10T10 Class.

In 1932, the overall permissible length for a two-axled single-deck chassis was increased to 27ft 6in, and to meet this the Regal's wheelbase was increased to 17ft 6in. It proved to be a popular chassis with company, municipal and independent operators, with London Transport's fleet of 718 representing about a quarter of the output. The preselector gearbox with fluid flywheel was an option.

Although most customers specified the six-cylinder engine, there was still a need for less powerful chassis. To meet this need a four-cylinder 5.1litre petrol engine developing 80bhp at 2,400rpm was introduced in 1930. Called the Regal 4, (model 642) it featured the long bonnet of the 6, and did not take advantage of the shorter length to give more bodyspace. An oil engine was introduced in 1933; this had a capacity of 6.6litre and developed 85bhp at 2,000rpm. Production totalled 177 up to the time the last one was built in 1938. They were sold to many corporations! Balfour Beatty Group (Mansfield District); BEF (City of

Oxford and East Midland); Dublin United Tramways, which had 40; SMT — the largest customer which bought 43; Provincial (Gosport & Fareham), who bought eight which lasted about 30 years!

In 1935 a redesigned, lightweight version was announced and called the Regal Mk II, model number 862. Unlike the Regal 4, it had a shorter bonnet enabling more bodyspace to be used. The engine was a six-cylinder 6.74litre unit which was available as petrol or diesel. This engine had a new development — wet liners, making their replacement easy. Although nicknamed the 'Bootlace engine' (when you pulled it hard, it broke), it reappeared in modified form in 1953 as the AV410. Further weight saving was achieved by having a 3/16in thick frame instead of the 5/16in section of the MkI — the resultant Mk II was about 0.5ton lighter. Sales totalled 104 with most having oil engines, although the last chassis — including eight for Sheffield United Tours in 1937 and 22 for Ribble in 1939 operated by Standerwick — had petrol engines. Other customers included Northern General, Rhondda, South Wales Transport and several Potteries independents. A normal control version was also produced called the Ranger (model 665) with a six-cylinder engine or the Mercury (model 640) with a four-cylinder unit. These were designed mainly for export and built between 1930 and 1939, although some were bought by home market customers. Timpsons bought both models in 1930 and 31 for its Grey Cars fleet in Torquay; these passed to Devon General in 1933, who bought two more Rangers in 1935 and eight more in 1938 — all being 26-seat coaches with petrol engines. Sheffield United Tours bought 10. A few more coaches were sold but only two became buses — those for Halifax Corporation with 26-seat Dick Kerr bodies. Three chassis were bought by Texas Oil Company for use as petrol tankers and another chassis became a horsebox. Only one four-cylinder oil-engined Mercury bus was built. This joined the Burton-on-Trent corporation fleet as a trial vehicle and, like the Guy buses it operated, had a Brush 26-seat body. Timpson retained four coaches in its London fleet after the sale of 18 to Devon General. The remainder of the 270 Mercury chassis were all lorries.

Left: *This coach with a Duple 31-seat body was one of 18 bought new by Elliott Bros (Bournemouth) Ltd in 1930, better known as Royal Blue. When it sold out to the Tilling Group in 1935, this was part of the fleet acquired by Hants and Dorset. Rebodied by Beadle as a 28-seater coach in December 1937 along with the other five of the batch, they were withdrawn in September, 1949. They all saw further service with various operators until 1956-8.* N. J. Treacher

Centre left: *Colchester's first AECs arrived in 1930, three Regents and this Regal with a Willett 31-seat body having two entrances. Withdrawn in 1947, it went to Thomas of Llangyrwyd, Glamorgan, who scrapped it in 1953.* Author's Collection

Below: *In 1931, East Midland bought 17 Regal buses and three coaches to add to the 77 AECs that it already operated. The buses had 32-seat front entrance bodies by Brush. This is one of four loaned to London Transport from October 1940 to August 1941; it was withdrawn in 1948.* D. W. K. Jones

Top: *Burnley Corporation's first AECs were six Regals purchased in 1931 with Roe 31-seat bodies which were unusual in having a double-deck type rear platform. In April 1933 three municipalities merged their fleets to become the Burnley, Colne and Nelson Joint Transport Committee. Withdrawn in 1950, this bus went for scrap.* Author's Collection

Above: *It appears that the AECs acquired from Elliott Bros must have been very reliable, as the new owner purchased 16 new ones in 1937 with 31-seat coach bodies, eight being bodied by Beadle and the others by Duple. This coach was burnt out in 1939 and it was returned to Duple for another body. The batch gave 20 years' excellent service.* AEC Ltd

Left: *Trent Motor Traction bought 50 AECs in 1937 — 20 being Regals of which five had preselector gearboxes. Duple and Willowbrook built the 35-seat bus bodies, many being converted to perimeter seating to take additional standees during the war. Most of the batch was rebodied by Willowbrook in 1950 as 35-seater buses but several were rebuilt by Trent like 712 which lasted until 1953.* N. J. Treacher

Centre left: *The Balfour Beatty Group ran a large number of AEC Regals and Regents in its bus fleets. This Midland General Regal was one of 17 bought in 1938. Although of the dual purpose type, 10 were 35 seaters and this was one of seven 32-seaters which lasted to 1959 — two years more than the higher capacity versions.* A. E. Jones

Below: *Mayne purchased its first AEC in 1928 — a Reliance that can be seen alongside the double-deckers. This view taken in 1937 shows that they must have been satisfied with the AEC bus, because five Regals and four Regents have been added to the fleet — the latter for the stage carriage service from Manchester to Ashton, a route it still operates.* Ian Allan Library

Right: *Enterprise and Silver Dawn was acquired by Lincolnshire Road Car Co Ltd in 1950. Having been an AEC customer since 1927 the bulk of its fleet was of this make. This 32-seat coach was the first of four bought in 1937 with Willowbrook bodywork. They were withdrawn in 1949 and bought by operators in Devon. This one went to Teign Cars who sold it in 1953 to Marston Coaches who ran it for a further four years.*
Ian Allan Library

Centre right: *The area around Halifax is very hilly, resulting in more powerful 8.8litre engines being specified. This is one of four delivered in 1938 with Park Royal bodies. Withdrawn in 1950, it went to Gillett Bros Co Durham and later it was sold to L&P, West Hartlepool.*   Author's Collection

Bottom right: *New in 1933 to Dutton of Mansfield with a 32-seat Brush body, this bus was acquired later by Hulleys of Baslow, who replaced the petrol engine by a 7.7 and subsequently had a utility Burlingham 34-seat bus body fitted. It gave them several more years of sterling service.*   R. N. Hannay

Left: *Of the 30 Regals with Weyman 35-seat bus bodies ordered by Glasgow Corporation in 1940, nine were diverted by the Ministry of Supply to other operators. This bus served Glasgow for 15 years before being sold to another Scottish operator who had a further four years' use before selling it in 1959. It ended up as a snack bar in Sowerby, Yorkshire.* N. J. Treacher Collection

Above: *Scottish Motor Traction bought 33 Regal 4s in 1934 with 34-seat bus bodies. This chassis originally had a Cowieson body but when photographed in 1958, it was owned by Lamcote, of Radcliffe on Trent, Notts and had received a 33-seat coach body built by Longwell Green. Lamcote acquired it from Lansdowne in 1956 and ran it until withdrawal in 1959.* D. M. Bailey

Left: *The eight Regal 4s bought by Gosport and Fareham in 1934 with 32-seat rear-entrance Harrington bus bodies had a lengthy life. Their 6.6litre oil engines were replaced by 7.7s in 1945 or 1946. This bus was one of a pair damaged by fire in 1957 and was rebodied in 1962 with a full fronted 35-seat bus body. When withdrawn in 1970 it went to a local boys' club.* N. J. Treacher

Right: *AEC offered a normal control version of the Regal called the Ranger. Over half the 101 produced were exported. This coach was one of a pair bought by Westcliff-on-Sea Motor Services in 1937 fitted with Duple 24-seat coachwork. Purchased by Grayscroft Coaches of Mablethorpe in 1952, it ran until 1961.*   E. A. Wain Collection

Below: *The largest order placed for the Regal Mk II was 25 for Northern General. Bodied by Weymann, the first 16 were 36-seaters and the remainder two less. The bodies were rebuilt by Pickering in 1946 and they were withdrawn in 1954/5.*   N. J. Treacher

Right: Eight Regal Mk IIs were bought by South Wales Transport in 1936. The bodies, seating 39, were built by Brush. They were withdrawn in 1949/50 all but two being scrapped, and these were not used as PSVs. C. Taylor

Centre right: Burlingham fitted 32-seat bus bodies on the five Regal Mk IIs for Cumberland Motor Services, thereby not taking advantage of the extra body space. Entering service in 1936 this bus served for 16 years before being sold to a contractor who kept it for six years. D. W. K. Jones

Below: Introduced in 1935, the 'Standard' Willowbrook body had nicely curved lines. Built on many types of chassis, this is one of nine mounted on Regal II chassis. It was bought by a member of the A1 Service — Ardrossan — in 1937, the only new one to go north of the border. Author's Collection

5 The Renown

With corporations considering replacing trams in the mid-1920s, larger capacity buses were needed. Thus the three-axled chassis came into being because it could be longer and consequently carry more passengers than a two-axled version. AEC had produced the LS class for London General in 1927, 11 double-deckers seating up to 70 passengers and a 34-seat single-decker. These were not really successful so a new chassis was designed by G. J. Rackham as a development of the Regent. Called the Renown, it had double drive and single tyres all round. The first entered service in the LGOC fleet in 1929. A 54-seater, on the model 663 chassis with an overall length of 27ft. It originally had a 6.1litre petrol engine, with was superseded in 1930 by a larger 7.4litre unit. Early 8.8litre oil engines were fitted into some of the LGOC's fleet of LTs as well as trials with the Gardner 6LW. Other variations included Lockheed hydraulic braking system, instead of the standard triple servo type, and Daimler preselector gearboxes before AEC began building its own under licence from Wilson.

The production of the 663 model totalled 1,250, all except the last 24 having double-deck bodies. These 24 were built in 1938 and had 32-seat coach bodies

Below: Of the 1,037 short wheelbase 663 Renowns, only four did not go into the LGOC fleet. Two of those were demonstrators, and one was dismantled. The odd one was bought by Northampton. One of the demonstrators was bodied by Brush in 1931 as a 58-seater and this became Birmingham City Transport No 92. In 1937, it became a recovery vehicle and in this guise it is seen pulling a Guy Arab out of Miller Street not long before its final withdrawal in 1961. N. J. Treacher

and 8.8litre petrol engines removed from LT class double-deckers. Of the remainder only three went elsewhere, these being demonstrators for AEC in 1931. One joined the Birmingham City Transport fleet and the second became Glasgow Corporation No 50. The remaining chassis was not bodied and was eventually dismantled.

The longer wheelbase chassis, model 664, was designed for 30ft long bodywork. The first two were built in 1930 for Warrington Corporation and had 65-seat double-deck bodies by Massey. They were followed by 50 35-seat single-deckers for the LGOC and subsequently a further 152 with similar bodywork joined them along with a 31-seat Harrington coach acquired with the business of Hillmans of Upminster. One other chassis received a 50-seat forward-entrance double-deck coach body in 1931 for Green Line services.

Orders from other customers totalled 143, of which one went to Australia, one to South Africa, six to Norway and 40 to Shanghai. Most of the others became double-deckers going to Eastern National (four) Doncaster Corporation (five), Thomas White & Co, Cardiff (five plus four in 1934 from Western Welsh), Bassett,Gorseinon (three), South Wales Transport (eight double-deckers in 1934 plus five single-deckers in 1933 with 13 more in 1939); Leicester City Transport bought nine double-deckers in 1939 with 16 following in 1940 which were the last to be built.

Below: The longer wheelbase 664 Renown was more popular for operation outside London. Amongst the small operators who bought them was the Ebor Bus Co Ltd of Mansfield, Nottinghamshire. This was one of a pair delivered in 1932 with Strachan 66-seat bodies. Author's Collection

Right: This view shows the impressive size of a 60-seat, forward entrance body built by Short Bros in 1933, for T. White & Co (Imperial) of Cardiff. This was the first of a trio which joined a similar bus purchased two years earlier. The fleet of 38 buses contained 30 AECs when the business was sold to Western Welsh in 1936. Nine Renowns were included and they lasted until 1951-3. A. B. Cross

Below right: The Weymann 39-seat body on this 664 Renown seated 39 passengers. Built in 1935 as a demonstrator and registered CMF 843, it was loaned to Coventry Corporation being numbered 176, and later, as shown, to Cumberland Motor Services. It was sold in 1938 to Valliant Coaches in London. Chris Taylor Collection

43

Above: *South Wales had both double- and single-deck bodies on 664 Renowns. Its last batch was 13 delivered in 1939 with 39-seat Brush bodies. This was one of two which lasted until 1954.* G. H. Truran

Right: *The last three-axle double-deck motor buses to be built for use in this country were 16 delivered in 1940 to Leicester Corporation with MCCW 64-seat bodies built to resemble nine constructed by NCME the previous year.* Author's Collection

6 The Q

In the early 1930s the country was in the depths of depression and both manufacturers and operators were looking for ways of economising. Manufacturers had reduced the cost of their product but were considering methods of increasing carrying capacities. With the latter point in mind, AEC produced a chassis with the minimum of intrusion to the engine by placing it behind the front wheel on the offside. The front axle of the chassis was set back and the entrance was behind it. A full front was fitted. Called the Q, the first was bodied by the LGOC with a 35-seat, centre entrance bus body and entered service in 1932. The chassis was powered by a six-cylinder 7.4litre petrol engine driving through a clutch and four-speed gearbox to the rear axle which had the differential on the offside. The chassis widened considerably after the

centre. Single tyres front and rear were used due to the even weight distribution. All subsequent Qs had a fluid flywheel and preselector gearboxes due to gear changing problems occasioned by the long linkage involved.

Shortly afterwards came two double-deckers of similar layout but having a shorter wheelbase with the front axle set further back. The weight distribution was a problem as twin rear tyres could not be fitted, so a larger size of single was used. The bodies took full

Below: *Leeds City Transport bought two 60-seat front entrance Q-type double-deckers with petrol engines in 1933 and 1934. This is the first and, like the second which was originally a demonstrator, it had an MCCW body.* Author's Collection

advantage of the repositioned power unit. The entrance was alongside the driver and the nicely curved outline looked slightly unusual because of a very short rear overhang. Sixty seats were provided and the complete bus weighed 6ton. Used as demonstrators initially, the first entered the Birmingham City Transport fleet in 1933 and had an oil engine fitted in 1934. The second bus was bought by Crosville.

With the growing interest in oil-fuelled vehicles a new, more compact engine was designed for the Q. Whilst based on the 8.8, but having a longer stroke and smaller bore, the capacity was 7.731litre. The first chassis to receive this engine was a demonstrator built in 1934 which entered the Leeds City Transport fleet. Only two more of the 23 double-deck chassis built had oil engines, another demonstrator and the last which went to Cardiff.

The first production single-deck Q chassis went to the Royal Blue fleet of Elliot Bros based in Bournemouth, with a 33-seat Duple coach body. Elliot Bros subsequently had three more, two seating 35 and one 37. Of the total of 319 built, 233 went to London Transport. Most of the others were bought by small operators, but Aberdeen Corporation purchased 11, Scott of Aberdeen four, Red and White four, South Wales Transport five, Imperial Motor Services of Abercynon seven, seven were exported to New Zealand and four to South Africa. Production ceased in 1936.

From 1934, an increasing number had oil engines and in the last 274 built, only Westcliff-on-Sea with three, Keith of Aylesbury and Summerbee of Southampton received petrol-engined chassis.

One other chassis was built. This was a three-axled version for the Green Line fleet in 1937. It had a centre entrance 51-seat double-deck Park Royal body. It did not prove to be successful and was demoted to bus duties. Withdrawn during the war, it went to Brown of Garelochhead and ended up as a van after that company had finished with it.

Below: Starting life as a demonstrator but with Grimsby Corporation in mind, this chassis was bodied by Roe with a central entrance 56-seat body and entered service in 1934. S. N. J. White

Above: *This is the second Q single-decker. Duple built the 33-seat forward entrance coach body for the Royal Blue fleet of Elliott Bros of Bournemouth, entering service in 1933. It was joined by a sister vehicle later in the year and two more in 1934. When the business was acquired by the Tilling Group at the beginning of 1935, the long distance routes were transferred to Western and Southern National. The excursion and tours business went to the local company — Hants & Dorset — along with the Qs.*
Author's Collection

Right: *The first oil-engined chassis were a pair which went to Suttons Crossley Coaches of Clacton-on-Sea in 1934. Duple built the bodies which accommodated 29 passengers in great comfort.* AEC Ltd

Bottom right: *Qs were bodied by a wide variety of coachbuilders. This 32-seat coach was a unique example constructed by Cravens in 1934 for Bevan and Barker of Mansfield, Notts.* Author's Collection

Above: *London Transport was the largest customer for the Q. This 1935 example has a Birmingham Railway and Carriage Works 37-seat centre entrance body. After sale by London Transport, it was purchased by an old folks home in Sutton Coldfield, Warwicks, and used until 1965 when it was bought by Mr Pick, then depot superintendent at the AEC Depot in West Bromwich, to save it from being scrapped. It subsequently returned to London and has been restored to its former glory.* R. N. Hannay

Left: *One of the longest lived Qs in this country was the example bought by J. H. Woolliscroft (Silver Service) in Derbyshire. The Willowbrook body seated 37 and the bus entered service in 1934. Seen here in 1958 it had had a grille fitted at the front to improve cooling of the engine. This vehicle has been preserved.* D. M. Bailey

7 Trolleybuses

AEC's first trolleybus (model 602) was built in 1922 using the straight framed 'S' type chassis for single-deck bodies. This was followed by a shorter wheelbase model (603) which had a set-back front axle, allowing a front entrance to be fitted — a quarter of a century ahead of similar motor bus designs. They proved very popular overseas with over 250 being exported in the next 10 years. Birmingham Corporation brought three of the double-deck 604 chassis which were similar to the 603. It also had one of the five 607s built — this being another double-decker but not having a set-back front axle.

It was the coming of G. J. Rackham that revitalised the AEC range. In 1930-31 the 663T trolleybus version of the Renown was ordered by London United Tramways which took 60. Trolleybus versions of the Regent, designated 661T, started production in 1931 with a pair going to Japan. In the following year ten were built — nine for Southend Corporation with low-bridge bodywork, and one high bridge bus for Bournemouth with that operator's standard dual doorways. The only customer in 1933 was Notts and Derby Traction Company which bought 15 with MCCW 55-seat bodies. Whilst the Southend buses had full front bodywork incorporating a radiator grille, the Notts and Derby buses had half-cabs. The only difference from the Regent was a wider flare at the top of the radiator to incorporate an English Electric badge above the AEC triangle. These were true 'diddlers'.

Production began in earnest in 1934 with a trial order for four from Portsmouth, a solitary chassis for LPTB and 36 for Bradford running over into 1935. By the time the last entered service in 1942 with Notts and Derby Traction, 380 had been built. Export markets were South Africa (Johannesburg, who took 19) and Australia (Adelaide with 21). Home customers were Reading (26), Portsmouth (another 85), Bradford (43 more), Cleethorpes (three), Notts and Derby (17), Brighton Corporation (12 in 1939 to open its trolleybus system), Brighton, Hove and District (eight, which did not enter service until 1946), Southend (six more in 1939) and 20 for Hastings Tramway Company as a start to replacing its first generation of trolleybuses.

A single-deck chassis (model 662T) was offered based on the Regal but a total of only 28 was built between 1932 and 1935. The 10 built in 1932 went to Notts and Derby Traction and, like its double-

deckers delivered a year later, had half cabs and radiators carrying the winged English Electric emblem above the AEC triangle. Darlington took eight in 1934 followed by three more in the following year but all these had conventional full fronted bodywork. The remaining seven went overseas, one to Italy (Milan), and six to Denmark (Odense).

The three-axled chassis related to the Renown was produced in two wheelbase sizes. The first short wheelbase 663T was built in 1930 as a demonstrator

Below: *The middle one of a trio of model 604 trolleybuses bought by Birmingham in 1926. Short Bros built the 51-seat bodies which had open staircases. They were withdrawn in 1932.*   B. W. Baker

and then sold to Southend Corporation. The second chassis was built in 1932 as a demonstrator for Birmingham City Transport also with an English Electric body; it was ultimately rebodied and became part of a batch of five delivered to Birmingham later in the year. The third chassis is also very interesting as it was sold to Bournemouth in 1933 with an English Electric 52-seat dual-entrance body. In 1936 it had the electrical equipment removed and was fitted with a petrol engine and gearbox becoming a Renown. In 1931 Walsall had two, but they followed what was to become standard practice, with a full front but a detachable, grille panel. The reason for this and the half cab was that the electric motor was mounted on the front of the chassis. Subsequent development resulted in more compact motors enabling them to be fitted under the floor. Of the remainder of the 89 built, two went to Australia (Sydney, to start its trolleybus system), three went to Canada (Edmonton), one trial bus went to Huddersfield, two to Portsmouth, 10 to Grimsby Corporation and one to LPTB.

Production of the longer wheelbase 664T chassis totalled 830. The majority of these went to London Transport including 18 built for Johannesburg in 1942 which could not be delivered because of the war. The first 10 went to Newcastle in 1935 followed by 11 more in 1937 and six in 1938. Rotherham, which had a single-deck fleet only, had seven 39-seaters in 1937 followed by four in 1939. Belfast Corporation bought two double-deckers in 1937 from AEC as well as trial chassis from other manufacturers. As a result AEC received a repeat order for 114, but because of the war only 88 were built. Chassis were exported to Russia (two), Canada (seven to Montreal), Australia (Sydney, 10), and South Africa (Durban, 14). The last

chassis ordered were ten to start the Cardiff trolleybus system, delivered between 1941 and 1943, the first service commencing on 1 March 1942.

Six more trolleybuses were built, one was a further three-axled model ordered by London United Tramways which entered service in 1933. It was the only 691T and had the highest seating capacity of any trolleybus in this country: seated in the central entrance LGOC body were 74 passengers. This chassis featured asymmetrical sidemembers, the nearside one being lower than the offside to give a low first step height. The other five chassis, based on the Q, received the designation 761T. The first was a 63-seater for Bradford, and the third had a 56-seat front entrance lowbridge body built for Southend. Park Royal fitted the fifth chassis with a 63-seat front entrance body in 1934. This bus entered service in Sydney in September 1934 and was joined by chassis two and four in 1936 and 1937 after being bodied by a local builder — Syd Wood. The Park Royal-bodied trolleybus was scrapped after an accident in 1948 but the other two lasted until 1957 and were the last Q type double-deckers in service in the world. Sydney had also received three Q motor buses in 1934. Originally petrol-powered they were converted to 7.7litre diesels in 1937/8 and were withdrawn eight years ahead of their trolley counterparts.

When production restarted after the war, a reduced market was anticipated at home and abroad. To obtain a larger share and to reduce costs, a new company was formed in conjunction with AEC's arch-rival — Leyland. Called British United Traction Co Ltd (BUT), AEC became responsible for home market vehicles and Leyland for export. For the former, two double-deck models were made: a two-axled and a three-

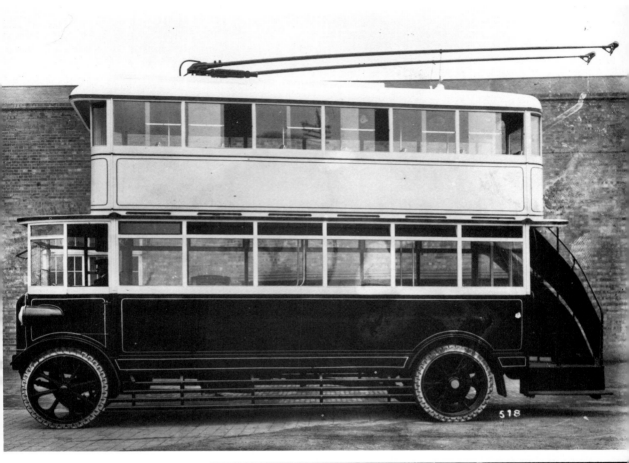

Left: *The first generation of single-deck trolleybuses had the motor mounted amidships giving a high floor level as shown by this view of a 603 model with a 37-seat Strachan & Brown body. These were unusual as they were actually built by ADC. There were three buses, all delivered in 1926 and withdrawn in 1938.* Author's Collection

Above: *The 607 chassis had a more conventional layout than the 604 but the Vickers body on this example for Birmingham only accommodated one more passenger at 52. Delivered in 1926, it was numbered 17 and was withdrawn when six years old.* B. W. Baker

Right: *Five of the trolleybuses replacing Birmingham's first generation were AEC 663Ts with 58-seat Brush bodies in 1932. These lasted eight years.* B. W. Baker

axled chassis. Production started at the Leyland factory in Kingston upon Thames where the Leyland Cub and Lynx chassis had been built before World War 2. When this factory was sold in 1948 production was transferred to Southall where it continued until the early 1950s when the Crossley works at Errwood Park, Stockport took over. The last home market chassis were built in 1958 — 90 two-axled 9613T models. Export chassis were built at Leyland until 1960 when BUT operations were centred on Scammell at Watford, the last chassis being produced in 1965.

The two-axled chassis was based on the Regent; originally coded 9611T, it had a overall length of 26ft. Its designation was subsequently altered, first to 9612T when the legal limit became 27ft, and later to 9613T for the 30ft version. Home customers included Ashton-under-Lyne, Bradford, Brighton, Cleethorpes, Darlington, Doncaster, Manchester, Nottingham, Portsmouth, Reading and St Helens Corporations. Glasgow was the sole purchaser of the 30ft version

and Notts and Derby Traction the only company operator.

While no three-axled motor buses were bought after 1940, the 9641T trolleybus version was popular usually carrying 70-seat bodies. They were bought by Belfast, Bournemouth, Cardiff, Glasgow, Huddersfield, Newcastle, Nottingham and Reading corporations plus London Transport. In addition Cardiff had a batch with single-deck bodywork.

Leyland had been responsible for the export chassis, but two modified versions of these were bought in the home market by Glasgow Corporation. The first was exhibited at the 1950 Commercial Motor Show, as was a 30ft long RETB two-axled chassis which was fitted with a 27-seat Weymann body and had a rear entrance behind the rear axle and an exit alongside the driver, forward of the front axle. This was later rebuilt as a 36-seater with the rear entrance removed and was joined by 10 more. These had 27-seat dual entrance East Lancs bodywork which, like the first, could carry up to 40 standees although this was later reduced to 30. The bodies were later modified to 36-seaters with a central entrance.

Glasgow's last trolleybuses were delivered in 1958 and were even more interesting as they again used the RETB chassis but with a longer wheelbase and an overall length of 35ft when the legal limit was 30ft. Special permission was given for their use on a tramway replacement route. Burlingham built the 50-seat bodies which had a front entrance and their surprisingly low weight of 8.25ton was only 1cwt more than the 30ft long versions. These were also the last BUTs to be built for this country.

Below: The author remembers this first sighting of Notts and Derby trolleybuses — the true 'diddlers'. To all intents and purpose they resembled their motorbus equivalents apart from having two poles on the roof and a larger badge on the radiator. This is one of 15 double-deckers with Weymann 55-seat bodies bought in 1933. Apart from their silence, they had a good turn of speed through the open country on the fastly timed 16-mile route between Ripley and Nottingham. They were withdrawn in 1949.
N. J. Treacher Collection

Left: *Southend Corporation bought the first 661T chassis for use in this country. The first batch of four was followed very closely by five more in 1932. An unusual feature of the 48-seat English Electric body was the lowbridge layout. Six more were bought in 1939 but these had Strachan 56 highbridge bodies.* N. J. Treacher

Centre left: *Bournemouth trolleybus system opened in 1933 with four experimental buses of which two were AEC, a 70-seat 663T and a 50-seat 661T, both with English Electric electrical equipment and bodywork. Both had their bodywork modified in 1934 when a separate exit was added losing eight and four seats respectively. As Sunbeam was chosen to supply further trolleybuses, both AEC chassis were fitted with petrol engines and gearboxes in 1936. In this form they gave another 14 years' service. This is the larger bus which was later acquired by Southend Corporation and made into a mobile convenience, before being scrapped in 1967.* G. O. Pearce

Below: *Apart from Notts & Derby the only other customer for the single-deck 662T chassis was Darlington Corporation which had eight in 1934 followed by a trio of which this is one, in 1935. Brush built the 32-seat body which had a central entrance.* C. Carter

Right: Excluding London United Tramways, Grimsby Corporation was the largest customer, for the 663T buying 10 in 1936. Roe built the 58-seat bodies which had a central entrance. Four of these were in the fleet when it was merged with Cleethorpes in 1957 but were withdrawn later in the year. J. C. Gillham

Below: After trying six different types of trolleybus in 1934 Portsmouth bought nine 661Ts in 1935 fitted with 50-seat English Electric bodies. They were joined by 66 more later in the year and 10 in 1937. Some of them lasted until the end of the system in 1963. N. J. Treacher

Right: The mountings of the trolleybuses on this English Electric 58-seat body were much more cumbersome than those used by other bodybuilders. This was a solitary 661T bought by Bradford in 1937, joining 36 bought in 1934/5. Another 41 similar buses arrived in 1938.   Ian Allan Library

Below: Rotherham's trolleybus system was beset by low bridges and double-deckers could not be used until the mid-1950s. This 39-seater English Electric-equipped Craven-bodied 664T was one of seven bought in 1937. They were withdrawn in 1949. Ian Allan Library

Above: *Cleethorpes Corporation bought three 661T trolleybuses in 1938 with Park Royal 56-seat bodies. With the curtailment of services at this seaside resort due to the war, they were sold in 1940 to Nottingham Corporation which ran them for 12 years.* Ian Allan Library

Left: *After trying seven makes of three-axled chassis when it opened the trolleybus system in 1938, Belfast Corporation placed an order for 114 AEC 664Ts but only 88 were delivered between 1940 and 1943 due to the war. A local coachbuilder, Harkness' built the 68-seater bodies.*

Left: *When Brighton Corporation replaced its trams in 1939, 44 AEC 661T trolleybuses were used. Brighton, Hove and District, as joint operator bought eight similar vehicles, all having Weymann 54-seat bodies, but due to the advent of war, they did not enter service until 1946. Most lasted until 1961.* N. J. Treacher

Below: *Bradford's trolleybus system was expanded in the 1950s under the guidance of a new general manager — the late Chacely Humpidge and many secondhand purchases were made from systems that were closing. Amongst these were the first eight 9611T's numerically, originally built for St Helens and entering service in 1951. When their system finished in June 1958, these eight went to Roe's for body overhaul and increasing the seating capacity of the East Lancs bodies to 63 from 56. They entered service for their new owner in 1959 and were withdrawn between 1965 and 1971. One of this batch has been preserved and repainted in St Helens livery.* Author's Collection

Above: *Cardiff's trolleybus system opened on 1 March 1942 with some of the last 10 644Ts to be built. These carried attractive Northern Counties 70-seat bodies and delivery was not completed until 1943. They were withdrawn between 1962 and 1965.* AEC Ltd

Top: *Newcastle Corporation bought 20 BUT 9641Ts in 1948 with MCW 70-seat bodies built to London Transport specification. A further 50 similar buses arrived in 1950. Many were in service when the system closed in 1966. A. M. Wright*

Above: *Although Glasgow introduced the last new trolleybus system in the UK starting with three-axled double-deckers in 1949, it was a pioneer of high capacity single-deckers. Using a 30ft long RETB1 chassis with an East Lancs dual-door body with accommodation for 27 seated passengers plus 40 standees. Originally they had a seated conductor by the rear entrance. Ian Allan Library*

8 The RT

London Transport engineers worked in close collaboration with their AEC counterparts for over 30 years after the two organisations became financially independent of each other. With the setting up of the LPTB in 1933 and their subsequent experiences in operating a wide variety of types, thoughts were given towards a better double-decker bus. They decided that a more powerful engine was required than they had at that time, but governed to run at less than its designed maximum ouput. To give the driver better control the preselector gearbox was adopted with air operation to reduce fatigue, and the gear selection lever was mounted on the left hand side of the steering column within easy reach of the wheel. The position of the gears was in a gate — not like the straight forward or

backward flick of a lever adopted by Daimler. Whilst traffic conditions were nothing like those experienced today, good braking was essential. As air was required to operate the gearbox, it was also used to operate the brakes.

The bus that resulted was the RT (model 0661), a fantastic vehicle that set the standards for the next

Below: *This is the first RT to be built for an outside operator and was intended to be exhibited at the 1939 Commercial Motor Show, but this was cancelled because of the war. Weymann built the 56-seat body, which had five bays unlike the neater LPTB design with four bays that became the pattern for postwar productions. It was withdrawn in 1956.* Ian Allan Library

Above: The early postwar Regent III, series 1 chassis were scattered far and wide. Five went to Rhondda in 1946 with provincial Weymann bodies. When withdrawn in 1958, they all saw further service, two for another six years, with other operators. G. H. Truran

Left: Ten RTs went north of the border in 1946 to join the Aberdeen Corporation fleet with 56-seat Weymann bodies. An additional seat was fitted downstairs in 1960. Whilst the body was a standard provincial type it gave a neater appearance than Birmingham's examples. Ian Allan Library

Bottom left: Birmingham City Transport had 15 RT chassis which received Park Royal 54-seat bodies, in 1947. These did not have the neat appearance of other Park Royal products. They were withdrawn between 1962 and 1964. N. J. Treacher

Right: The RTs bought by St Helens Corporation were to full LTE specification including the Park Royal body. When fully equipped with blinds, they were unusual in using the main aperature for the route number and the intermediate points appeared on a smaller blind. Fifteen were delivered in 1950 and a further 25 in 1952. AEC Ltd

two decades and a model that was to serve London faithfully for 40 years. The engine was larger than any of its competitors, having a swept volume of 9.6litres which could develop 120bhp at 1,800rpm, but was derated to 100bhp, to give economy and good engine life. It was flexibly mounted in the chassis and drove through a fluid flywheel to a remotely mounted gearbox and thence to an underslung worm rear axle. The driver's cab received a lot of thought and even included a sliding door! His position was slightly higher than on a Regent and had a much better view, particularly to the nearside which was greatly assisted by a lower positioned radiator and bonnet. Life of the moving components on the chassis was greatly enhanced by the use of an automatic chassis lubrication system.

The prototype entered service in July 1938 carrying an old open staircase body removed from a Leyland Titan TD1 whilst a new body with an equally modern specification was built by the LPTB at Chiswick. When this was nearing completion, the old body was removed in January 1939 and the new body was completed in April. The new bus started a new class, the RT, one that was to total 4,825 by the time the last one was built in 1954. While not all were in service together, and there was a gap of eight years caused by the war between the first production batch entering service in 1940 and the arrival of the next batch, the last examples were not withdrawn until March 1979, one of which was ostensibly a 1948 vehicle.

'Prewar' production was 152 chassis, all but one going to London Transport in the early part of the war. The odd one was intended to be exhibited at the 1939 Commercial Motor Show. It was bodied by Weymann and joined the Glasgow Corporation fleet. In 1940 AEC hired RT19 from London Transport. Various modifications were made to the chassis which became the prototype for the postwar production; it was repainted green and demonstrated to various operators, being returned in 1942. When Southall resumed PSV production after the war a start was made on fulfilling London Transport's prewar orders. The model was given a new code — 0961. There

were, however, shortages of buses throughout the country and allocations were made to the needy by the Ministry of Transport. London Transport decided, on the grounds of standardisation and interchangeability, that the bodies would be constructed with the aid of jigs and this delayed the start of building. As a result many RT chassis were reallocated to other operators including Devon General, Rhondda Transport, West Riding and the corporations of Aberdeen, Birmingham, Coventry, Douglas, Grimsby and Halifax. The output of the 9.6litre engine had been increased to 125bhp at 1,800rpm but the London versions were de-rated to 115bhp.

Bodywork on these provincial RTs varied greatly, the West Riding ones carried Roe central entrance bodies, others were bodied by Weymann and Park Royal to their standard designs. The Coventry example did not enter service until 1950 and the MCW body on this was more like the standard RT. St Helens however ordered 15 RTs in 1950 with Park Royal bodies to full LTE specification. Whilst using the standard destination layout, these differed in that the route number appeared in the large aperture, and intermediate points went where LTE put its route number. 25 similar buses joined them in 1952 of which 21 were purchased by Kingston-upon-Hull corporation on their withdrawal from service by St Helens in 1962.

There has never been a vehicle to equal the RT for reliability and longevity. Whilst London Transport's high standard of maintenance has contributed to this, it is interesting to note that many of its rear-engined replacements themselves have been withdrawn from London service when between three and nine years old. Fortunately a large number of RTs have been preserved to keep the legend alive for many decades to come.

Above: *London Transport had 4,825 AEC RTs and by 1955 had achieved complete standardisation on this model by AEC or Leyland for its double-deck requirements apart from 76 Regent III series 2, with lowbridge bodies. Service reductions resulted in the prewar models being withdrawn in 1955 followed by the non-standard Craven-bodied examples in the following year. These were quickly sold to large and small operators throughout the country and very often served them longer than LTE. This is one of two that entered service with Harper Bros Ltd of Heath Hayes in 1957 and was withdrawn in 1967.* N. J. Treacher

Left: *Further service reductions in London resulted in more RTs being withdrawn with older Park Royal and Weymann bodies. These again rapidly found buyers who included Bradford Corporation taking 25 to assist its tramway conversions.* Author's Collection

9 Postwar Regents

The postwar Regent was called the Mk II, although it was basically the same as the model produced just prior to the war but with a triple servo braking system — a vacuum hydraulic was the previous standard — and louvred bonnet sides that were used on the 'unfrozen' chassis. The power unit was the direct injection '7.7litre' unit (actually 7.58litre) coupled to a four-speed 'crash' gearbox. The first bus to enter service in this country was a Weymann 56-seat bodied example for Mansfield District Traction who placed an order for 10.

The chassis series was 0661, numbers continuing after a gap from the unfrozen chassis. It should be pointed out the AEC allocated chassis numbers to orders. If the numbers were reduced or cancelled, they periodically reallocated the missing numbers. As a result some operators received new chassis with lower numbers than some in service. Altogether 695 Mk IIs were built with the last entering service in 1948 for Reading Corporation. One large customer was Liverpool Corporation who had 100, South Wales Transport (41), Trent Motor Traction

(55), and City of Oxford (20). Other customers were Kingston-upon-Hull Corporation, Tynemouth & District, Enterprise and Silver Dawn, Midland General, Western SMT, Cardiff Corporation, as well as smaller operators. The first 50 chassis, however, were exported to India.

One order of interest was placed by Midland Red for 100 which were supplied without canopies and had a block-type radiator. They were bodied by Brush and MCCW who fitted full width frontal structures, similar to that Midland Red had built on its D1 which entered service in 1944 and which set the standard for the next decade or so. These buses entered service during 1948-49.

Below: *The 13 Regent Mk IIs delivered to Western Welsh in 1946 were extremely unusual in having ECW bodies to its prewar design, seven of these being 56-seat highbridge versions. They were all withdrawn in 1959, with only one going for further service.* C. Taylor Collection

Above: *A regular customer for almost 40 years, Liverpool bought 100 Regent Mk 2s 1946 and 1947. This is one of the last batch of 42, all having Weymann framework which were panelled and trimmed by Liverpool. All seated 56 passengers. Whilst this bus was withdrawn in 1962, the last members did not depart until four years later.* G. F. Ashwell

Left: *Midland Red's initial postwar production was of underfloor-engined chassis, so it bought 100 Regent Mk IIs for its double-deck requirements. These were supplied without bonnets and had a block-type radiator so that a modern frontal structure could be fitted. Bodywork was shared by Brush and MCCW seating 56 and they entered service between 1948 and 1950. They were withdrawn between 1961 and 1963.* N. J. Treacher

Above right: *The last 10 Regent IIs were ordered by Reading Corporation with 52-seat lowbridge Park Royal bodies, arriving in 1948. Two were withdrawn in 1962 and the remainder in 1964.* N. J. Treacher

1947 saw the introduction of the Regent Mk III series 2. The most noticeable feature was a deeper chromium-plated radiator and a much neater bonnet arrangement. The louvres were deleted and the split was about level with the top of the wing. Below this was a bulge to clear the dynamo. The upper part sloped down from the rear to the front and was hinged alongside the driver's cab and had a spring to assist lifting and holding it open for maintenance. The wings were deeper with the bottom edge tapering downwards from the front, outer edge to cover the end of the chassis frame. Whilst the frontal structure was very imposing, it was not as compact as that fitted on the RT, on which the new chassis design was based. A choice of engines was available — the 9.6 developing 125bhp at 1,800rpm or the 7.7 developing 98bhp at 1,800rpm. Transmission was either through a clutch to a four-speed crash gearbox or via a fluid flywheel to a four-speed preselector gearbox having a column-mounted change like the RT. The wheelbase was 16ft 4in for 26ft long bodies but 27ft long bodies could be fitted when allowed from June 1950.

From January 1948 a new series of designations was used. Number 68 indicated when the bus was fitted with the 7.7 engine. Number 11A indicated a vacuum-braked chassis with crash gearbox 26ft long (later changed to 12A). 13S indicated vacuum brakes and synchromesh gearbox on a 27ft long bus. If the prefix was 96, the larger 9.6litre engine was fitted,

and an E suffix indicated a preselector gearbox. Number 12 indicated 26ft long bodies, and 13 was used for 27ft versions. The A model had the D124 sliding mesh (crash) gearbox.

Following a demonstration for Trent in 1949 with a Crossley double-decker, an order of 10 Regent IIIs with Crossley synchromesh gearboxes was placed; these vehicles were designated 9612X. The AEC synchromesh unit (D166) which had been fitted into various Regal and Regent chassis experimentally since 1949 became and option in 1952. Many operators converted their D124 gearboxes to D166 specification to improve their reliability. Whilst the first 7.7-powered chassis entered service in 1948 as a batch of 75, by the time the last was built, in 1957 for Reading Corporation, total production was only 136. Most went to municipalities but York Pullman bought four, Rhondda Transport 10, and the most unusual order was for six going to a Tilling Company — Hant & Dorset in 1948 — with NCME lowbridge bodies. These, however, were originally ordered by Western SMT.

The chassis with the 9.6litre engine was much more popular with over 3,000 of the Series 2 being built, many going overseas. Home customers included BET companies, corporations, Scottish Bus Group and independents. Generally the preselector versions were bought by corporations.

With the growing popularity of the 'new look' front, which Crossley had produced in 1949/50 for Birming-

Left: *Sunderland Corporation had six early Regent IIIs with 9.6litre engines and Roe 56-seat highbridge bodies in 1947.* AEC Ltd

Below: *One of Eastbourne's smart fleet of Regent IIIs with East Lancs 52-seat highbridge bodies, this example was one of four that entered service in 1948. Their seating was increased by two in each saloon in 1960. They were sold in 1966.*
N. J. Treacher

Right: *A most unusual purchase for a Tilling company was six Regent IIIs with 7.7litre engines and Northern Counties lowbridge bodies seating 53 passengers delivered in 1949. These buses were originally ordered by Western SMT.* N. J. Treacher

ham City Transport, AEC offered it as an alternative, the first being built for Devon General in 1952, and exhibited at that year's Commercial Motor Show. Its appearance was virtually identical to the BCT version with elongated slots in the detachable front panel. Later Bradford and Kingston-upon-Hull specified this for their 1953 orders, whilst Liverpool designed their own, which used a detachable grille that was wider than the BCT pattern, bearing a close resemblance to Midland Red's design.

At the 1954 Commercial Motor Show, a new double-deck model was introduced as the Regent Mk V. The Mk IV designation had not been announced officially, but had been given to an underfloor-engined chassis built in 1949 and bodied by Crossley with a full fronted 60-seat body. Unlike the Regal Mk IV, the Regent Mk IV's front axle was not set back and did not offer any advantages over the orthodox chassis, but was more difficult to maintain. The vehicle was shown to a large number of operators but was not put into service. It was rebodied by Park Royal who managed to reduce the unladen weight but the project was abandoned, possibly due to stability problems.

The first Mk V was powered by the new AV470 engine which developed 112bhp at 1,800rpm. Transmission was either by a four-speed synchromesh gearbox, or Monocontrol — a direct acting epicyclic gearbox used in conjunction with a centrifugal clutch. Braking could be achieved by air pressure or vacuum. The new model had a redesigned frontal structure having a more curved bonnet top and shallower front panel which incorporated an oblong black mesh grille with a thin chrome surround which was slightly curved at the top and bottom. A central chrome strip had the

AEC triangle mounted at the top whilst the model name was on a small oblong plate at the bottom. A similarly shaped grille was used on goods vehicles. This new frontal structure was fitted on some later production models of the Mk III range. Whilst the alternative of the exposed radiator was available, only a few Mk V chassis were so equipped: they were known as the M (medium weight), D (double-decker), 3 (synchromesh gearbox), R (right-hand drive), V (Vacuum brakes). The 2 (Monocontrol transmission) was only available with air brakes. It had a 16ft 4in wheelbase and could be 7ft 6in or 8ft wide. Designed as a lightweight model to replace the 7.7litre powered Regent III, it weighed about 4ton 2cwt and was intended for a gross weight of 10.5ton. Production ended in 1959.

This model was soon joined by a more powerful version using the 9.6litre dry-liner A218 engine (of the Mk III) with an output of 125bhp at 1,800rpm and a torque of 430lb ft at 1,000rpm. Similar braking and gearbox alternatives were offered but the chassis was 13cwt heavier than the MD3RV with a further 2cwt being added if Monocontrol transmission was called for. Surprisingly the 8ft wide model added 2cwt more. Gross weight was a maximum of 12ton. If more power was needed the 11.3litre engine was used. It developed 150bhp at 1,800rpm — but this was only used on export chassis. Another option on the 'heavier' model was Gardner 5LW 94bhp or 6LW 112bhp engines. However, only the latter was fitted, the customers being Aberdeen (5), Glasgow (75) and Rochdale Corporations (40). The Aberdeen and Glasgow buses had a slightly different grille, being similar in outline without a chrome surround and having vertical slots instead of a mesh. The 8ft wide model became standard soon afterwards but 7ft 6in wide chassis could be built in 'economic' batches.

At the 1956 Commercial Motor Show, an 18ft 7in wheelbase chassis was introduced to carry 30ft long bodies that had recently been authorised. Two examples were shown, one for an independent — Cotterills of Micheldean — and the other (for Western Welsh) with a fully-automatic gearbox driven through a centrifugal clutch. Both had rear entrance Park Royal bodies with doors — the one for Western Welsh having a detachable roof. This new model had a designed gross weight of 13.5ton resulting in larger tyres and heavier springs increasing the weight to 5ton with the synchromesh gearbox. Originally coded

LD, it became 2D from 1959 for the 590-powered chassis irrespective of wheelbase

A new engine based on the wet-liner AV470 was introduced in 1958. Known as the AV590, it was the same size and power unit as the 9.6litre engine it displaced. Chassis so fitted became a series 2 and had that number as a prefix to their designation.

A new range of goods vehicles announced at the 1964 Commercial Motor Show featured new engines. They were dry-liner units the 187bhp AV691 having a capacity of 11.3litre and a larger 203bhp 12.47litre unit, the AV760. This resulted in the AV590 being superseded by the AV691 but derated to 128bhp at 1,800rpm and the chassis prefix changed to 3.

With the Government introducing a Bus Grant scheme to improve the efficiency of bus operation by furthering one-man operation, the rear-engined double-decker was favoured, and as 25% of the vehicle's cost (later increased to 50%) was paid for by the Government, demand for front-engined chassis decreased and the last Regent was delivered in 1969 — 40 years after the first.

Below: Based in Sparkford, this Somerset operator bought this 9.6litre engined Regent III with a 55-seat Duple lowbridge bodywork in 1949. N. J. Treacher

Right: *It was a tradition for many years to have a local bus on the Roe stand at the Commercial Motor Show. This was their 1950 exhibit a Regent III bearing Crossley badges built to the recently authorised length of 27ft, seating 56 and finished in the dark green livery that had just been adopted. Note the polished aluminium bonnet which was a feature of Leeds buses. It was broken up after being sold in 1969.* Author's Collection

Left: *Edinburgh bought 17 Regent IIIs with 9.6litre engines and preselector gearboxes in 1950 — a surprising order as its last AEC had been allocated a decade earlier. The Brockhouse bodies were 56-seaters, another unique purchase. Sold in 1960, they appear to have been scrapped, as no further user has been found.* N. J. Treacher

Right: *Trent's last new AEC double-deckers were 10 8ft wide Regent IIIs with 9.6litre engines and 56-seat Willowbrook bodies. They were unique in having Crossley synchromesh gearboxes. No 1204 is seen shortly after delivery in the summer of 1950 in Derby bus station.* R. N. Hannay

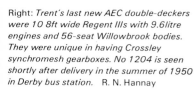

Left: *The last bodies built by Northern Coachbuilders in 1950 went on 40 Regent III chassis for Newcastle Corporation. Seating 56 passengers they gave over 16 years' service. This bus has been preserved.* G. H. Truran

Below: *City of Oxford Motor Services Ltd was a loyal customer for AECs for about 40 years for all its requirements. The Regent III has Park Royal 53-seat lowbridge body and was one of seven new in 1952. Alongside is a 32-seat Willowbrook-bodied Regal Mk 3 new in 1949, one of a batch of 20. All had 9.6litre engines. The double-decker was withdrawn in 1965 and the single-decker in 1961. Both went for further use.* N. J. Treacher

Right: Exhibited at the 1952 Commercial Motor Show, this was the first of 100 Regent IIIs with synchromesh gearboxes delivered in 1953-1955, all but two having Crossley bodies seating 56. The frontal structure was also built by Crossley to Liverpool Corporation's design which resembled the Birmingham 'new look' pattern but was wider. 51 were still in service in December 1969 when Merseyside PTE took over. Author's Collection

Below: This Regent MK III was the first to have a 'new look' front. Exhibited at the 1952 Commercial Motor Show, it had a synchromesh gearbox, a prototype Weymann Aurora lightweight body and seated 58 passengers. When withdrawn in 1965, it went to Edmunds of Rassau. Author's Collection

Above: *Kingston-upon-Hull Corporation
bought its last new AEC double-deckers in
1953. This is one of the six which had
58-seat Weymann bodies and 9.6litre
engines. They were amongst the first
production chassis to have the new look
front, and were 16-19 years old when taken
out of service.   AEC Ltd*

Left: *With the acquisition of many small operators in 1951-3, PMT found itself short of double-deck buses. To assist it received 12 Regent IIIs with 58-seat NCME bodies in 1953, the chassis having been ordered by two of the firms taken over — Tilstone's and Stoke Motors. Originally delivered in a drab all red paint, they received a more attractive livery when repainted as shown. They were taken out of service between 1965 and 1967.*
N. J. Treacher Collection

Top: *The Regent Mk IV was never offically announced. It was based on the Regal Mk IV with an underfloor engine. Crossley built a 60-seat body and although it was demonstrated to operators throughout the country it did not enter production.*
Author's collection

Above: *Exhibited at the 1956 Commercial Motor Show, this LD2RA was one of the first 30ft two-axled double-deckers to be built. The Park Royal body seated 73 and had a removable top, but it was never operated as an open topper.* G. H. Truran

Above: *The bar in Beverley has a Gothic arch with a nominal height of 10ft 9in which straddled the main road. To get double-deckers through, a special contour was adopted until the bar was by-passed. This Regent V, a 590 with Monocontrol, was one of a pair of 66-seat Roe buses purchased in 1957. Both were withdrawn in 1972 with this bus disappearing but its sister has been saved for preservation.*   Author's Collection

Right: *In 1957 16 Regent Vs entered the City of Oxford fleet. This is one of five with 61-seat Weymann bodies. It was withdrawn in 1969 after an accident and was purchased by the Oxford Bus Preservation Group which converted it to open top. It was sold in 1970 to a customer in the Bahamas.*   G. H. Truran

Above: *When larger double-deckers were authorised, East Kent wanted more powerful vehicles, leading it to buy Regent Vs with 590 engines. Its first batch totalled 40 delivered in 1959 with 72-seat forward entrance bodies by its usual bodybuilder — Park Royal. These were unusual in having full fronts. In the next eight years a further 121 were purchased but having half cabs.* N. J. Treacher

Left: *Another operator to have Regent Vs with exposed radiators was Leeds City Transport. This batch totalled 14 vehicles with MCCW 71-seat bodies delivered in 1960. They were the last exposed radiator buses to enter the fleet.* G. H. Truran

Left: *Bartons passengers have had a high standard of comfort even on double-deckers. The external appearance also received consideration. This batch of six Regent Vs delivered in 1960 was the first in the UK to have wrapround windscreens. Northern Counties built the 70-seat lowbridge bodies.* Author's Collection

Above: *Due to height restrictions in the area of Llanelly docks, which precluded the use of underfloor-engined buses, South Wales bought six Regent Vs with 590 engines and 37-seat Roe bodies in 1963. Withdrawn in 1972, three were purchased by Bedlington and District, Northumberland, which withdrew them in 1974. This one has now been preserved. With two similar buses bought in 1959, these were the last front engined, half cab single-deckers to enter service in this country.* N. J. Treacher

Left: *Devon General's operation of AECs ended in August, 1980 with the withdrawal of its last Regent Vs. Amongst the last to survive was this example from eight with 69-seat Willowbrook bodies bought in 1964.* R. N. Hannay

10 Postwar Regals

When the plans for the single-decker were formulated towards the end of the war, it was christened the Regal Mk II. However it was soon realised that there had been a Mk II before the war, so it was renamed Mk I and stickers were affixed in the brochures to ammend them. Like the Regent Mk II, it had a louvred bonnet side and triple servo braking system. Its classification was 0662 starting with chassis No 24001, the first 167 chassis being exported. Whilst numbers were usually given to customers' orders as they were placed, the initial postwar chassis production was allocated by the Ministry of Transport who had controlled wartime production. The first one went to Venture Transport followed by three for George Ewer (Grey-Green), all with Duple coach bodies. The first large batch followed soon after with 10 for Newcastle Corporation going to Harrington for bus bodies; these were some of 18 consecutive chassis sent to this builder, three of which were coaches for Robin Hood Transport of Nottingham.

Altogether 1,665 postwar Regal Mk Is were built, of which about a quarter were exported. Home customers included Alexanders, SMT, many BET companies, Red and White Group, Northern Ireland Road Transport Board, Balfour-Beatty Group and a large number of independents.

In 1948, an improved chassis appeared called the Mk III, based on the provincial version of the Regent Mk III. The 7.7-powered chassis was numbered initially in an 0682 series but later it was amended to 6821 with an 'A' suffix when the four-speed sliding mesh gearbox was fitted, or 'X' for a batch of 20 with Crossley synchromesh gearboxes for Trent Motor Traction, who incidentally also had the first 12 Mk IIIs which received Windover coach bodies. Production totalled 763 chassis of which over 40% were exported. As for the Mk I, customers came from all over the country. BET companies, Balfour Beatty Group, SMT and Alexanders took the majority, some were purchased by the Tilling Group for the Southern and Western National companies plus Crosville. Many independents also bought the Regal III, with some taking 30ft long versions with the last entering service in 1954.

The initial designation when the 9.6litre engine was fitted was 0962; this became 9621 with the suffix A to indicate sliding mesh gearbox, E for preselector or S

for synchromesh. The last chassis were built in 1956 by which time the total was 1,728 and, surprisingly, the percentage exported was the same as the 7.7litre model. AEC was a very large earner of foreign currency with their products having an excellent reputation for reliability and performance, in the 1945-75 era.

The first order for this model was placed by Halifax for 13 buses. Again BET companies were good customers as well as the Balfour Beatty Group, Great Northern Ireland Railway, Alexanders, Red and White Group, many went to independents including West Riding, a few more went to municipalities. London Transport, who had 50 Regal Is, bought 30 Mk IIIs. A longer-wheelbase version became available in 1950 to accommodate 30ft long bodies, but with the advent of the underfloor engine chassis, sales of vertical engined models to the UK dwindled in the early 1950s although they continued overseas.

Below: *The first large batch of postwar Regals went to W. Alexander, in 1946. Of 30 purchased, 20 went to Burlingham for 36-seat bus bodies. This bus became part of the fleet transferred to W. Alexander and Sons (Midland) Ltd, on the splitting of the fleet in 1961 and was sold as a non-psv in 1964.* N. J. Treacher

Above: *An unusual conversion to 'open top' was carried out to three 1946/7 Regal Mk I buses with Beadle 36-seat bodies, when withdrawn in 1957/8 for use on seafront services in Hastings. This gave them another 20 years' life.* N. J. Treacher

Left: *With a shortage of buses and coaches after the war a multitude of bodybuilders sprang up. One which is in existence today and is part of a larger organisation is Wadham which made this 32-seat coach for Direct Coaches of Birmingham in 1946. It was later owned by the London Brick Company.* AEC Ltd

Right: 'MacBraynes for the Higlands' was the
slogan and a Highland Warrior its emblem.
Today their routes are operated by the smart
vehicles of Highland Omnibuses. This was
the second of nine with Park Royal 35-seat
coach bodies bought in 1947. It was sold in
1960 to a contractor.   R. N. Hannay

Above: Whilst Bristol met the needs of the
Tilling companies it could not supply enough
in the early postwar years, resulting in
chassis coming from other sources. Crosville
bought 12 Regal IIIs with 7.7 engines in
1947 with Strachan 35-seat bodies
resembling the ECW product. Six similar
vehicles went to each of the Southern and
Western National fleets.   N. J. Treacher

Right: Maidstone and District bought 55
Regal III coaches with 7.7litre engines in
1948/9. All had Harrington coach bodies,
some being off prewar chassis. Of the new
bodies, five had full fronted bodies of a type
designed for export. These were withdrawn
in 1962/3.   N. J. Treacher

BODY BY EASTERN COACH WORKS LTD LOWESTOFT

Lough Swilly

YELLOWAY

Top left: *Another unusual combination was the fitment of ECW bodies on AEC chassis. This 35-seater, one of four, looks smarter than the average product for the Tilling fleets due to a more imaginative colour scheme.*   AEC Ltd

Centre left: *The first home market customer for the 9.6 litre Regal III was Halifax Corporation with a batch of 12 having 32-seat Roe bus bodies new in 1949. Ten more arrived later in the year. Withdrawn between 1962 and 64, most went for scrap.*   AEC Ltd

Left: *Yelloway Motor Services Ltd, was a loyal AEC customer right up to the end of production in 1979. This attractive 33-seat coach with Trans-United bodywork entered service 30 years earlier. It had a 9.6litre engine.*   Author's Collection

Top: *Eire allowed two-axled single-deckers to be 30ft long before the UK. The Great Northern Railway (Ireland) bought 30 Regal IIIs in 1948 with Park Royal bodies, the first 23, like this one, having 39 bus seats and the others coach seats and a full width canopy. The GNR(I) fleet passed to CIE on 1 January 1959 and this bus ran until 1965.*   W. Montgomery

Above: *Gelligaer UDC took delivery of four Duple 35-seat buses on 9.6litre engined Regal III chassis in 1949.*   Author's Collection

Left: *With acquisition of several private operators in the early 1950s, the Potteries fleet had a wide range of chassis and body types. This Regal Mk III had a 35-seat bus body by a local builder (Lawton) and was one of a pair bought in 1949 by Stoke-on-Trent Motors which sold out in 1951.*
N. J. Treacher

Centre left: *The Robin Hood fleet is no longer in existence, but its name is still carried on Barton vehicles. This is one of its many AECs but the first to have a full fronted body. This 35-seater 9.6litre Regal Mk III was built by Burlingham in 1949 and looked much smarter than the prototype shown at the 1948 Commercial Motor Show for SMT. It had been sold by the time Barton bought the business in 1961.* N. J. Treacher Collection

Below: *Several operators were acquired by Eastern Counties in 1951. The largest was B. Beeston & Son, East Bergholt with 16 vehicles which included this Regal III with a 35-seat Duple A coach body bought in 1949. Withdrawn in 1957 it was later bought by Charlton-on-Otmoor Services in Oxfordshire. Eastern Counties had replaced the 9.6litre engine with a 7.7 in 1952.* R. N. Hannay

Left: *Everingham Brothers of Pocklington used the Regal III with pre-selector gearbox as the basis of this 35-seat Harrington bus body in 1950. The fleet was acquired by East Yorkshire Motor Services Ltd in 1953 which ran this bus until 1962. This bus had originally been built for West Bridgford UDC.* AEC Ltd

Right: *The Gurney-Nutting 33-seat coach body on this Regal III bears a resemblance to the Duple design of the period apart from the ugly frontal treatment. Wrights of Southend purchased the coach in 1950.* Author's Collection

Below: *This unusual design was an attempt to increase the seating capacity of coaches within the overall length of 27ft 6in. This body accommodated 43 on two levels in forward and rearward facing seats. It was built in 1950 by the Lincs Trailer Company to a design by Mr George Crellin on a Regal Mk III chassis with a 9.6litre engine and preselector gearbox. The owner was Granville Tours (AE Blackbourn) of Grimsby. It was only 10ft 6in high.* Author's Collection

Below: Gliderways of Bearwood, West Midlands bought this 30ft long 9621A Regal in 1951. It had a 37-seat Harrington coachbody featuring Harrington's patent dorsal fin which gave it a distinctive look. Author's Collection

Bottom: Doncaster Corporation bought the last three 30ft long buses with Roe 39-seat bodies in 1953 when most other operators were running under floor-engined buses. Three similar vehicles went to the Belfast Steamship Co of Liverpool. Converted to one-man operation in 1958 Doncaster withdrew its examples in 1965. One of this batch has been preserved. Author's Collection

11 Regal Mk IV

Just before World War 2 began, an AEC underfloor-engined chassis was sent out to Canada. War deferred developments on this idea until 1948 when two more chassis were built; they were bodied by Park Royal, one seating 40 and the other 38. The first was registered UMP 227 and testing was carried out in conjunction with London Transport. The second proto-type, originally registered VMK 271, was sold to Douglas Corporation and became NMN 255 in 1951.

By the time the Regal Mk IV was announced the Construction and Use Regulations had been amended to allow 30ft long buses on two axles. Two more prototypes were built to this length, but the first production vehicles, ordered before the alteration, were 25 27ft 6in long 35-seat buses for London Transport. The first 30ft models were six for the 1950 Commercial Motor Show, including one in City of Oxford livery with a 42-seat Willowbrook body registered OJO 730. This was subsequently bought by Douglas Corporation and re-registered NMN 201.

The Regal Mk IV's power unit was a horizontal version of the 9.6 which had a fluid flywheel and pre-selector gearbox with air pressure operation for the brakes. The chassis code was 9821E or 9821LT for London Transport. The original chassis was designed to be integrated with the body, but later a deeper, self supporting frame was introduced — being re-coded 9822E with preselector gearbox or 9822S with the synchromesh alternative that became available. Of the 2,672 produced, 503 went for export and of the ones remaining in this country, London Transport had 700, some of which were operated until 1979 — a length of service almost equal to the RT. It should be pointed

Below: One of the 1950 Commercial Motor Show exhibits was this Regal IV with a 39-seat Windover coach body, going to Sheffield United Tours. It was joined by five more for the 1951 coaching season to run alongside Regal Is and IIIs. MWJ 197 ended its days working for Hulleys of Baslow. Authors Collection

out that, in addition, AEC also built a large number of left-hand drive chassis for export.

The Scottish Bus Group used the Regal Mk IV on their express services to London. Alexander built the 30-seat bodies which had a toilet compartment. For their normal tours, other coaches seating 38 were bought. Whilst the BET group ordered chassis, the majority of theirs and the independents who collectively bought the bulk of all the home market chassis, had coach bodies fitted — LTE bought 15 with rather ungainly ECW 39-seat coach bodies, and five similar coaches went to Tillings Transport — the only ones that were ordered by the nationalised Tilling Group.

Very few bus bodies went on the Regal Mk IV (apart from the LTE examples): Rochdale, Ipswich, Dundee

and Doncaster Corporations, City of Oxford, Western Welsh, GNR (Ireland), West Riding and Hanson were the major operators of buses. One other interesting use for the Regal Mk IV was by British European Airways who had 37-seat half-deck bodies with large luggage lockers built by Park Royal for their services to Heathrow Airport from their terminal in London.

The last chassis ordered by home market customers were two old customers both specifying Plaxton bodies having central entrances — Glenton Tours and Wallace Arnold. The former is the only firm to have this type of body today. This was not the end of the Regal Mk IV as it continued to be produced in both right- and left-hand drive versions for export up to the mid-1960s. It was then replaced by a Mk VI version.

Above: *St Helens first underfloor-engined bus was this Regal Mk IV with a dual door 42-seat Roe body delivered in 1951. It was unusual in having the entrance at the rear and exit at the front.* Authors Collection

Right: *Originally one of six Regal Mk IVs bought by Tillings Transport in 1951 fitted with rather ugly 39-seat ECW bodies similar to the 25 London Transport RFW class. They were later rebodied by ECW with what came to be the standard coach body fitted to the Bristol MW. Seen at Clovelly on Silver Jubilee Day 1978, it was then owned by Denver Bros.* R. N. Hannay

Bottom right: *Neath and Cardiff Luxury Coaches Ltd was founded in 1929 to run a service between the two towns. In 1947 it started a body building company called Longford Coachworks. This was its first body on an underfloor-engined chassis and accommodated 39 passengers. Entering service in 1951, it was joined by two more in the following year. They were withdrawn in 1962. The company was acquired by the BET in 1953 and passed into history when South Wales Transport and Western Welsh took over the vehicles and services on 1 January, 1971.* AEC Ltd

Right: *One of the most pleasing designs on underfloor-engined chassis was the Wayfarer produced by Harrington. This example for Hadwins Luxury Coaches of Ulverston, Lancs, seated only 33 when delivered in 1951. Hadwins was purchased by Barrow Corporation in 1971 but was resold in 1977 to another coach operator — Shaw of Silverdale.* Author's collection

Centre right: *With the advent of the underfloor-engined chassis, bodybuilders had a free hand with styling, resulting in some curvaceous designs. This Bellhouse Hartwell body had a central entrance and accommodated 41 passengers and was bought in 1952 by an operator in the Manchester area. The chassis had a preselector gearbox like most Regal IVs.* Author's Collection

Below: *Weymann 44-seat bus bodies were fitted on four Regal Mk IVs with preselector gearboxes for Dundee Corporation in 1953. This bus was converted to dual-door layout in 1956, losing three seats in the process.* AEC Ltd

Left: *Creamline Motor Services (Bordon) Ltd,
Hampshire used a pair of Regal Mk IVs with
synchromesh gearboxes on leave services
provided for troops as well as stage carriage
services. This one has the first coach body
built by Mann Egerton and had 43 seats. The
Regals were delivered in 1953.*
Author's Collection

Below: *Willowbrook had a lot of regular
customers in the counties surrounding its
Leicestershire factory. One of these was
Silver Service which bought two Regal Mk IVs
with 41-seat coach bodies in 1953. They had
centre entrances which was the fashion of
the period and preselector gearboxes.*
Author's Collection

Left: *Amongst the 150 buses acquired from
GNR(I) in 1959, most of which were AECs,
were 33 Regal Mk IVs with GNR bodies built
on Park Royal frames. This dual purpose
40-seat bus was new in 1955 and lasted for
17 years.* W. Montgomery

12 The Reliance and Monocoach

In the early 1950s passenger traffic was beginning to decline due to the removal of petrol rationing and the consequent growth of car ownership. Labour costs were also beginning to rise — the underfloor-engined chassis helped operators by increasing the numbers accommodated in a bus by 25%. Economies had to be looked for in other directions. Reducing the weight of the bus would assist fuel consumption — it was considered that one ton reduction gave another mile per gallon — as well as lessening wear and tear on brakes, tyres, etc. Within two years of announcing the Regal Mk IV, active development work was being carried out on a successor — the Reliance. Introduced in 1953, it was a completely new model, having virtually only the wheelbase in common with the Regal Mk IV.

A new smaller power unit was designed, based on the prewar upright six-cylinder 6.75litre engine used in the Regal Mk II. This was a wet-liner unit, unlike all other AEC engines which were of the dry type, and this enabled engine overhauls to be carried out more quickly and simply. The new engine was available in two sizes, the AH410 and AH470, with capacities referred to in cubic inches, the 410 equalling the 6.75litre of the prewar unit and the 470 being a larger 7.58litre to replace the dry-linered 7.7. AEC used the alphabet as a prefix code for chassis components for unit type and part numbers — engines were prefixed A, gearboxes D, up to Y for chassis frames and Z for miscellaneous. The second letter in the engine designation was H for horizontal or V for vertical.

To assist performance and economy, a five-speed, direct drive top, synchromesh was standard with the options of 5.22:1, 4.7:1 or 4.08:1 enabling a high top speed to be achieved with the latter ratio without losing efficiency through indirect gearing. At the other end of the performance scale, steep gradients could be climbed easily due to a 6.25:1 bottom gear. On a trip on an early North Western Reliance using the Motorway, 16.1mile/gal was obtained with a top speed of 65mph. An interesting point was a full glass of water on the front dash from which not a drop was spilled. It also had a lively acceleration, reaching 60mph from a standing start in 60 seconds.

The braking system had a total lining area of 618sq in giving excellent stopping power, with actuation by vacuum or air pressure. With the air braking system, an alternative gearbox was offered — a direct-operating epicyclic type called Monocontrol.

Below: The first production Monocoaches were built in 1954 for Scottish Omnibuses, seating 45. This is the last of the batch of six (B425-30) which was followed by 50 more entering service at the end of the year and continuing into 1955. They subsequently purchased the Reliance with similar 45-seat bodywork. B430 was withdrawn in 1969 and was scrapped. Author's Collection

This dispensed with the clutch pedal, the change being effected by moving a small lever through a gate mounted close to the steering wheel. Most customers, however, specified the synchromesh unit.

A new type of chassis designation was introduced — this indicated M (medium weight), U (underfloor), 3 (synchromesh gearbox), R (right-hand drive), and V (vacuum brakes). Alternatives were 2 (Monocontrol), A (air brakes), and L (left-hand drive).

The rear axle was a spiral bevel type and, coupled to a lighter front axle and chassis frame, the overall weight of the chassis complete with the 25gal fuel tank full was around 3ton 17cwt — about a ton lighter than the Regal Mk IV. Body builders also had weight-reducing exercises enabling the unladen weight of a 44-seater bus to come down to 5.75ton from around 7.5-8ton.

At the same time as the Reliance was being developed, a chassisless version was under way at Park Royal. The prototype emerged in 1953 as a 45-seater powered by the AH470 engine but interestingly having a centrifugal clutch and pre-selector gearbox. Registered NLP 635 it was finished to London Transport's specification and painted in Green Line livery, running initially in conjunction with two other makes against RFs. The Monocoach, as the new model was called (although it was a bus), weighed 5.5ton — 2ton less than an RF. After it was returned to AEC, it was used for further development before being sold to West Monmouthshire Omnibus Board in 1957. A second prototype was built later in 1953 seating 44; it had a deeper windscreen which became standard. The unladen weight of 210 AMP, as the vehicle was registered, was 5ton 7cwt, about 8cwt less than a Reliance with a similar body.

Due to the British operators' conservatism and desire for a freedom of choice for bodies, the Monocoach only sold in small quantities although some customers bought Reliances with Park Royal bodies. Possibly a bigger weight difference might have helped sales but it is difficult to see how this could be achieved. Total production of the MC totalled 188 — all being model MC3RVs with five-speed synchromesh gearboxes and vacuum brakes. The first order was for six 45-seaters for Scottish Omnibus in 1954 and the last in 1957 for six 41-seat dual purpose vehicles for Highland Omnibuses, these however being bodied by Alexander who constructed 75 of the total. Scottish Omnibuses had 39 in 1956/7 like the Highland semi-coaches and Alexanders took 30 buses seating 45 in 1955. The other customers were Northern General (25 44-seat buses), Alexanders (20 45-seaters delivered in shell form to Alexander Coachbuilder), Scottish Omnibuses (50 in 1954/5 as 45-seater buses), and Sheffield Joint Omnibus Committee (two 40-seat semi-coaches and three 44-seat buses in 1955). The remaining buses went to Laycock of Barnoldswick, one in 1954 and another two years later. Booth and Fisher (now swallowed up by South Yorkshire PTE) had two 45-seaters in 1954, one of which has been preserved. Willowbrook surprisingly made two vehicles in 1954, one of which was the only one to live up to its name. Seating 41 it was used by AEC as a demonstrator and was subsequently sold to Morley of Edwinstowe, Nottinghamshire. Its sister was a 44-seat bus being sold in 1955 to West Monmouth-

Below: Walter Alexander bought 20 Monocoaches in 1954, all but one being built by Park Royal, as 45-seaters differing in external trim from the SMT buses. Transferred to the new Midland fleet in 1961 it was withdrawn in 1970. G. H. Truran

Above: *This was one of two Willowbrook Monocoaches built in 1954. Both were used as demonstrators by AEC. This 45-seat bus was bought by the West Monmouthshire Omnibus Board in May 1955 and was sold in 1967. The Board also purchased in 1957 the prototype Monocoach NLP 635.* A. E. Jones

shire OB, after AEC had also used it as a demonstrator. The remaining 'chassis' is even more interesting as it went out to Australia entering service in 1959 with a dual-door 41-seat bus body by Coachmaster!

Between 1955 and 1958 UTIC — a co-operative in Portugal — imported 150 sets of material for the MC3LA model (left-hand drive, synchromesh gearbox and air brakes). Seating capacities varied between a 39-seat coach and a 43-seat dual door semi-coach. UTIC subsequently built many more chassisless buses and coaches in the 1960s and 1970s using Reliance running units.

Sales of the Reliance were widespread. Operators liked its performance, liveliness and economy. The 470 engine did, however, suffer from cylinder head gasket failure, but this was eventually cured. It sold in greater quantities than its rival, the Tiger Cub. Whilst it did not benefit from bulk orders from the BET, it nevertheless appeared in the fleets of the majority of its constituents and was popular with independents and municipalities as well. The AH410 engine was specified by a few operators including Aldershot and District as well as East Kent, Grimsby-Cleethorpes Corporation and Scottish Bus Group. As the only differences were pistons, liners and fuel pump setting, the majority of these were later converted to the 470. In 1960 experiments began with rotary fuel pumps and this became standard in 1963. As well as improving the liveliness of the engine, it returned better mile/gal. In response to a limited demand for a smaller chassis, a 13ft 7in wheelbase version was produced for Jamaica in 1958 with other examples going later to Cyprus, West Indies and Europe.

In 1961 the overall length for PSVs was increased to 36ft and AEC were the first manufacturer to offer a chassis. Two models were available, one — the 4MU3RA — having the AH470 engine. The more powerful version used the 9.6litre AH590 engine derated from 180bhp to 153bhp at 2,000rpm. This model had a six-speed ZF synchromesh gearbox as standard but Monocontrol was an option and was coded 2U3RA or 2U2RA respectively.

In 1966 the AH410 and 470 engines were replaced by a dry-linered AH505. This had a capacity of 8.14litre and developed 145bhp at 2,200rpm. The standard gearbox was a six-speed AEC constant mesh unit having an overdrive top gear, which had been introduced in the Mercury and Marshal goods chassis in 1962, and had become available on the Reliance with the 410 or 470 engines in 1963. Both the 30ft and 36ft models were coded 6MU3R or 6MU2R respectively — the option of vacuum brakes having been discontinued. The 9.6litre 590 was replaced by a larger dry-linered engine. The 2U3RA Reliance had the 11.3litre version fitted — the AH691 — which was set to develop a similar output to the 590-157bhp at 2,000rpm. Buses could now be allowed up to 12m (39ft) in length and a longer wheelbase was offered to take advantage of it. The model type became 2U3ZR, the 3Z indicating the ZF gearbox in six-speed form for coach chassis or four-speed for stage carriage operations, if a six-speed constant mesh gearbox was fitted the designation became 2U4RA or 2U2RA with Monocontrol transmission. A 4 prefix indicated air suspension and an 8 coil springing. A five-speed version of the Monocontrol gearbox entered production in 1967 making it suitable for coaching purposes when fitted with a 3:1 rear axle ratio as it gave a top speed of 70mph. An early customer for this unit was

PMT, who also specified coil springs, the model being 8U2R.

In AEC trucks from 1964 two engines were available in most of the heavy range. Like the relationship of the 590/690 units, the 691 (11.3litre) and the 760 (12.47litre) were substantially identical with differing pistons and liners and the smaller engine having a rotary fuel pump and the larger an in-line unit. As operators called for the larger engine in increasing quantities, the 691 version was discontinued in 1973. This affected the Reliance in that its power unit became an AH760 set to develop a lower maximum output.

By this time most customers were buying the Reliance in 11 and 12-metre forms. This was the only PSV model being built at Southall but was selling well at home and overseas. Unfortunately a process of rationalisation by Leyland decreed that individual marques would disappear as new models were introduced. This resulted in the letters AEC disappearing from trucks and on 25 May 1979 the AEC works was closed. There were a number of unfinished Reliance chassis at that time and these were slowly completed. It is interesting to note the large number of operators, particularly independents, who placed Reliances in service in 1979-80, many not having purchased 'heavy' chassis previously. Green Line increased its last order to give them time to evaluate a replacement. It will be interesting to see who gains the business of the loyal AEC users!

Below: Devon General retained the Grey Cars fleetname of the Timpson subsidiary acquired in 1933, for its coach fleet until the setting up of the National Travel and merger of coaching interests. Delivered in 1955 this Reliance 37-seat coach was one of a pair with Weymann Fanfare coachwork. They were transferred to the associated Greenslades fleet in 1964.   Author's Collection

Right: Black and White's first AECs were some prewar Regals purchased secondhand. In 1956 it bought its first new ones in the form of 10 Reliances with Willowbrook 37-seat coach bodies. This is seen when new on the occasion of an Omnibus Society visit to the Cheltenham headquarters. Over the next eight years a further 24 were purchased but 12 years then elapsed before a final order for 11 36-footers was placed.   R. N. Hannay

Below right: Finished in the light blue livery of Europabus — a network of railway-associated operators covering services from London to various destinations on the continent — this coach belongs to the English constituent, East Kent. One of 16 similar vehicles (most were finished in East Kent colours) it has a 37-seat Beadle body. In the same year, 1957, 35 other Reliances also with Beadle bodies joined the fleet. They were withdrawn between 1972 and 1976.   Author's Collection

Top: *Surprisingly Aldershot & District bought only one underfloor-engined Dennis, which arrived in 1951. All subsequent large single-deckers were AEC Reliances. This example was bought in 1957 and is one of 30 with Weymann 43-seat bus bodies.*   N. J. Treacher

Above: *Greenslades Tours Ltd of Exeter was a loyal AEC user in postwar years. Amongst the Reliances bought were two in 1957 having Harrington coach bodies, one seating 28 for Continental tours and the other 37 for use mainly in this country. The business was acquired by the BET group in 1953 and after various changes of policy by National Bus Company is now being used again as the fleetname for its Exeter coaching activities.*   Author's Collection

Top right: *Baxters of Airdrie standardised on Reliances in 1954 and also bought some Regent Mk V double-deckers. This Reliance was new in 1958 and has a 41-seat Alexander body and the Regent following was one of a pair placed in service in December 1957 with 55-seat Massey lowbridge bodies. Baxters sold out in December 1962 to Scottish Omnibuses which proceeded to integrate the buses in its own fleet but met such a lot of public opposition that the separate identity was retained for many years.* Author's Collection

Right: *In postwar years, few coaches were built by Roe, but this Reliance was one of a pair bought by a former Derbyshire independent who became a subsidiary of South Yorkshire PTE. Delivered in 1958 the body uses the shell of the bus-type but has roof quarter lights, tinted panels in the front dome, coach seats and the destination box mounted below the windscreen.*   Chas H. Roe

Top: *Brewers Motor Services of Caerau, Glamorganshire has a fleet of about 30 buses and coaches and AEC have featured in it for several decades. They were unusual as an independent operator to buy Weymann bus bodies, eight 44-seaters being purchased between 1954 and 1963. This bus was new in 1958.*
N. J. Treacher Collection

Above: *Scottish Omnibuses also used the Reliance for touring. Of 49 delivered in 1959 20 had Alexander 41-seat bodies like this one. B673 was one of the first to be withdrawn in 1973 and was purchased by Tarmac. Altogether 293 Reliances were bought new between 1955 and 1966. AEC Ltd*

Right: *Another fleet that has disappeared is Thomas Bros (Port Talbot) Ltd, which added these three 36ft long Reliance 470s in 1963. Marshall built the 53-seat bodies which were unusual in having illuminated advertisement panels. The fleet of 41 vehicles (including 22 Reliances) was taken over by South Wales Transport Co Ltd in 1971. Authors' Collection*

Right: *North Western became an AEC fan in the 1950s placing several orders for Reliance coaches and dual-purpose vehicles. This is one of a batch of 20 delivered in 1961 with a 43-seat Willowbrook dual-purpose body. It is finished in an attractive red and cream livery with a black roof and window pillars. The 20 buses were divided between Trent, Crosville and Selnec in 1972 with the dispersal of services. Author's Collection*

Centre right: *Park Royal was not noted for luxury coaches, but one of its regular customers — East Kent — purchased 20 in 1962. The basic shell was that of the bus body but its shape was altered by a destination-less roof dome, new grille and mouldings allowing a re-styling of the livery. The 46-seaters were based on the 36ft long 490-powered Reliance chassis; the total cost to standard specification was £2,975 for the latter plus £3,625 for the body. If a 470 chassis was specified, the total was £275 less at £6,325. 519 FN was one of 10 rebodied by Plaxton in 1973 with Panorama Elite III 49-seat coach bodies.*
Author's Collection

Left: *After having three new double-deck coaches in 1950 and a solitary Reliance in 1959, Premier Travel's purchases were secondhand vehicles. A change of policy came in 1964 when two new 36ft long Reliances with 49-seat Alexander Y type coach bodies were purchased; each year from then until 1979 similar purchases were made. This is one of the 1964 order. Author's Collection*

Below: *The Alexander Y type body is one of the classic designs of recent years. This 49-seat example is one of 56 bought by the Scottish Omnibuses fleet in 1966. It was one of six sold to Highland Omnibuses in 1973 following 10 bought four years previously. R. N. Hannay*

Above: *The Executive Express service conveyed passengers direct from the air terminal to the aircraft. Eight Reliance 590 coaches with 49-seat Duple bodies were bought in 1966. They were operated on BEA's behalf by LTE and when the service was discontinued, four coaches were transferred to Glasgow (Abbotsinch) airport services. They were withdrawn between 1974 and 1976.* N. J. Treacher Collection

Right: *One of the problems facing the smaller bus operators in recent years has been obtaining bodies to their requirements. When one of the few remaining independents in the Potteries ordered this Reliance 590 chassis in 1967, Willowbrook increased the bodies that it was building on Leopards for Midland Red by one to fit on it. They were of the dual purpose type seating 49.* R. N. Hannay

Bottom right: *South Wales bought its first Reliances with Monocontrol transmission in 1968. These were its last large engined Reliance buses. Willowbrook built the 53-seat bodies. This is one of five delivered in a modified livery. The vents in the roof are for a heating and ventilating system developed by South Wales which these five vehicles had.* G. H. Truran

Right: *Edmunds Omnibus Services Ltd, has a modern fleet of around 12 vehicles. It is based in Rassau near Ebbw Vale, Monmouth, and was a keen user of AEC buses. This 1972 Reliance has a 505 engine, six speed synchromesh gearbox and 45-seat dual purpose Willowbrook body.* G. H. Truran

Centre right: *Following the disastrous fire which destroyed the Blue Bus fleet and depot in 1976, five new Reliance 760s with Plaxton bodies were purchased soon afterwards as replacements for that fleet by Derby Corporation. This coach has bus doors for use on stage carriage work and qualify for a grant towards its purchase.* G. H. Truran

Below: *Although the production of Reliances ceased in 1979, many were not placed in service until 1981. One of the last went to Abbey Coachways Ltd of Selby, Yorkshire fitted with a Plaxton Supreme IV Express 53-seat coachbody, and was built to the maximum legal length of 12 metres.* G. H. Truran

13 Integral and Low Height Double-Deck Designs

By 1954 London Transport had an almost standard fleet of RTs which were most satisfactory. However, they were not content with this and work proceeded on a better vehicle to replace the LT trolleybus fleet. This was unveiled at the 1954 Commercial Motor Show as the Routemaster. It carried eight more passengers than the RT and yet weighed only 6.75ton, a saving of 0.75ton. The 9.6litre engine was similar to the RT, but hydraulics were used to operate the brakes and gear change; an improved ride was given by independent suspension for the front wheels and coil springs or later air suspension at the rear which helped stability. The weight-saving was achieved by dispensing with separate chassis and using aluminium alloy for the body structure and panelling. Much thought had gone into maintenance of the vehicle. To reduce removal time for overhaul, the engine, front suspension and steering were mounted on a subframe with a similar arrangement for the rear axle and suspension. A second prototype with an AV470 engine was built, followed by two more with Leyland O600 engines, one bus built by Weymann and the fourth as a Green Line coach by ECW.

Production started in 1958 by Park Royal who had carried out the initial design work, with the AV590 engine as standard but, later on, Leyland 600s were fitted to certain batches. The weight had increased to 7.25ton — still over a ton lighter than equivalent conventional buses. Subsequent developments resulted in the RML — a 30ft long version having a 2ft 4in bay inserted in the middle seating 72 and weighing 7.75ton. Coach versions for Green Line were also made, short one seating 57 and long ones 65.

At the 1962 Commercial Motor Show, a forward entrance 30-footer was exhibited as RMF 1254. When it subsequently entered service it did so on BEA services, who also bought 65 27ft 6in long forward entrance buses which towed luggage trailers. Northern General ordered 50 30ft long forward entrance buses with Leyland 600 engines, and these were joined by RMF 1254 which was re-engined to match. Northern General had very good service out of these buses and some were acquired by London Transport on their withdrawal in 1979/80, for further non-PSV use, joining the ex-BEA vehicles. Altogether 2,875 Routemaster were built.

It looks as though the Routemaster is going to be around for many years yet, seeing off newer rear-engined types. Whilst surely nothing can surpass the RT for longevity and reliability, the Routemaster is going to be a good second.

AEC and LTE considered a replacement for the RM to enable one-man operation of double-deckers. Using some components of the Routemaster it had a transverse rear engine and four-speed semi-automatic transmission. Entering service as FRM 1 in 1966, it was still in use in 1981.

At the same time as the Routemaster was being evolved thoughts were given to a low height design. This work was undertaken by Crossley in Stockport. Again a chassisless vehicle emerged with sub frames at the front and rear. Coil springs were used for the suspension but later air springs were used at the rear. The braking system was unusual in having hydraulic actuation for the front brakes and air for the rear. The engine drove through a four-speed gearbox down to enter the dropped centre rear axle on the nearside. The two prototypes had an AV470 engine but all subsequent buses had the AV590.

Inside the bus a full width rearward facing seat covered the protrusion of the gearbox. A sunken lower deck gangway enabled a full length centre gangway to be incorporated upstairs as well within an overall height of 13ft 4in. Upstairs there were 41 seats and 31 downstairs. The first vehicle was exhibited at the 1956 Commercial Motor Show in Walsall's colours and the second, although registered by AEC, eventually joined the Birmingham City Transport fleet, appearing as a demonstrator at the same show. The code for these was MB3RA with the M being omitted on subsequent buses which had the larger 590 engine.

In 1960 a forward entrance version entered production. This necessitated a rearrangement of the drive line to go down the offside of the structure. To achieve this a transfer box was fitted behind the engine allowing the gearbox to be mounted further over, under the staircase. The seating capacity, like the rear entrance model, was normally 72 but with two more seats upstairs and two less downstairs. The designation given was 3B3RA and this also applied to the 27ft 8in long version seating 65 built for City of Oxford. Production of the Bridgemaster ceased in 1963 by which time 180 had been built. The first five

Left: *The Routemaster prototype introduced at the 1954 Commercial Motor Show had the radiator mounted underneath at the front to keep the vehicle within the maximum legal overall length of 27ft and it entered service in 1956 after extensive testing in this form. When the overall length was increased to 30ft for two-axled vehicles in 1956, RM1 was fitted with a more conventional radiator which resulted in the grille being extended 4in forward. It is seen here in October 1958 after modification.* G. H. Truran

Below: *Cardiff Corporation bought six 68-seat short Bridgemasters in 1960 fitted with platform doors. One was dismantled by the Corporation and the others went to Newton of Dingwall, Scotland in 1972.* G. H. Truran

were built by Crossley, the last being supplied as a skeleton to be finished off by Harkness for Belfast Corporation. The remainder were built by Park Royal following the closure of the Crossley factory. Customers included Corporations, BET companies and independents and Scottish Omnibuses (ordered by Baxter of Aidrie).

As sales of the Bridgemaster were disappointing, again possibly due to operators wanting freedom of choice for bodywork, a separate chassis was developed, the prototype, 7552MX, having a 71-seats forward entrance Park Royal body. This had a Bridgemaster frontal structure but on subsequent chassis it was set slightly lower. The new chassis was called the Renown and coded 3B with the option of Monocontrol (2) or synchromesh gearbox (3); RA (right hand drive, air brakes) completed the designation. The wheelbase was 18ft 3.5in with overall lengths of 30ft or, with a shortened rear overhang, 28ft. Only the AV590 engine was offered and this was set in the chassis at an acute angle to the offside enabling the synchromesh gearbox to be coupled to it directly without interfering with the staircase, with the drive going to the offside of the dropped centre rear axle. Whilst air suspension was used on the rear axle, the front reverted to a beam axle with leaf springs.

The first five production chassis were bodied by Willowbrook followed by 15 Park Royal 71-seaters for South Wales Transport. Although designed for forward entrance bodywork, the next four chassis for Leigh Corporation had 72-seat rear entrance bodies built by East Lancs. It's interesting to note that out of the 252 built, 128, had Park Royal bodies giving a combination similar to the Bridgemaster! Eight chassis went to independents, one to Scottish Omnibuses (in place of a Bridgemaster ordered by Baxter) with BET companies (South Wales, Western Welsh, East Yorkshire, North Western and City of Oxford) and Leicester, Leigh, Nottingham, Rotherham and surprisingly Wolverhampton Corporations being customers for the others. The last five entered service in 1967.

Below: *East Yorkshire was the largest operator of the Bridgemaster. Its first batch of four arrived in 1960 as 76-seaters with platform doors; these went for scrap in 1976 having given longer service than the 44 delivered in the following three years.* AEC Ltd

Right: *Whilst it was quite common in the 1930s for manufacturers to build demonstrators for specific operators, it has not been so common since the war. Having built a rear-entrance Bridgemaster for Birmingham which was purchased in 1956, a forward-entrance version four years later after being tried, remained as a demonstrator until sold to Osbornes of Tollesbury, Essex.* G. H. Truran

Left: *Smiths of Barrhead (owned by the Scottish Co-operative Wholesale Society) followed its purchase of two Bridgemasters with a pair of Renowns in 1963. Park Royal built the 74-seat bodies. When the business was sold in 1968, they were bought by Barton Transport Ltd.* AEC Ltd

Below: *This was the last of 18 Renowns purchased by North Western in 1963. Park Royal built the 74-seat forward entrance bodies. When transferred to Crosville in 1972, these reliable buses went back to running their long routes in preference to rear-engined chassis. They were withdrawn in 1978.* R. N. Hannay

Left: *The smart fleet of King Alfred of Winchester added two Renowns with 75-seat Park Royal bodies in 1964. These went to Hants and Dorset in 1973 when it bought the business.* G. H. Truran

Right: *In spite of its advanced features, the only customer other than LTE for the RM type was Northern General which bought 50 Leyland 0600 powered forward entrance buses in 1965 and later the prototype RMF 1254. Many of the buses withdrawn in 1979/80 found their way back to London.* AEC Ltd

Left: *The last frames to be built at the Weymann works at Addlestone were fitted on five Renowns for Wolverhampton Corporation the home town of Guy Motors. The bodies were completed by MCW at Saltley and the 73-seat buses entered service in 1966, passing to the West Midlands PTE in 1969.* D. E. Smith

14 Rear Engined Single-Deckers

Whilst only one rear-engined double-decker was made, the story of the single-decker was very different. The rear horizontal engines were mounted longitudinally driving down the chassis, coupled directly to a direct-acting epicyclic box, which in turn drove via a prop-shaft, a hypoid bevel rear axle of the Reliance type but turned round. With the 8.2litre AH505 engine, the Swift weighed only 4ton 8cwt It was offered in two versions — a straight frame for coach work and one with the frame dropped forward of the rear axle enabling a low entrance for bus work. In reality only the latter was built, having either a 16ft 6in wheelbase for a 33ft long body or an 18ft 6in version for 36ft long buses, the code being MP2R.

Announced with the Swift at the 1964 Commercial Motor Show was a more powerful version, called the Merlin (model 2P2R) using the 11.3litre AH691 which developed 157bhp at 2,000rpm. Due to it being a

Below: At the 1966 Commercial Motor Show, one of the two exhibits for Leeds City Transport was this Swift 505 with a Roe 48-seat dual door body. It was the first of 10, the remainder arriving in the following year, followed by 40 in 1968, 50 in 1969 and 20 in 1971. The last two batches had 691 engines. Leeds City Transport was integrated into the West Yorkshire PTE in 1974.
Author's Collection

longer engine than the 505, it was only available with an 18ft 6in wheelbase. When production commenced, both models were sold as Swifts but LTE used the original designations. By the end of 1967 over 1,000 Swifts had been sold, customers included several corporations, independents and BET companies. It was also popular overseas, particularly Australia, and in chassisless form, UTIC built the mechanical components into monocoque bodies, the last going in 1979. Vehicles from 1973 had an AH760 engine derated to 165bhp at 2,000rpm.

Rear-engined chassis were generally more troublesome than their mid-mounted contemporaries, although the Swift survived longer than its companions using the same chassis frame — the Leyland Panther and Panther Cub, — and production came to an end in the mid-1970s for the home market, due partly to Leyland's decision to rationalise bus production on one model — the Leyland National. The last two Swift chassis were built for Red Rover of Aylesbury who specified synchromesh gearboxes. The last vehicles to enter service however were three for Grimsby-Cleethorpes Corporation in 1976.

AEC's last passenger design was shown at the 1968 Commercial Motor Show, and was the most powerful ever offered in this country. Appearing in left-hand drive form, the Sabre featured a rear-mounted V8 engine of 12.2litre capacity, developing 247bhp at

2,600rpm with a torque of 580lb ft at 1,400rpm 60% more power than the 505-powered Swift. The engine had been developed by AEC to give high performance, life and reliability for high-speed operation — ideal for overseas markets. The five-speed semi-automatic gearbox had a direct drive top gear which when used with the lowest ratio available gave 75mph. Suspension was by coil springs. With a lining area of 832sq in the air operated braking system was more than adequate for the vehicle. The frame was flat topped, for coach work (not produced for the Swift) and while it was offered for bus work, no mention was made of a low-frame version.

At the 1970 Commercial Motor Show a home market version was shown complete with a new-style ECW coach body. This attracted a lot interest but only the one was built for use in this country and was still in existence in 1980. The main reason for its discontinuance was that the V8 engine, also used in goods chassis, did not live up to the standard of reliability of the in-line engines. So ended AEC passenger designs.

Moseleys of Loughborough, the enterprising coach dealers introduced Continental bodywork into this country in the late 1960s. The builder — Caetano — came from Portugal where UTIC, a co-operative of several bus operators, had been assembling AEC chassis and building bodies for a number of years. They had evolved an integral coach called the Tagus which used Swift components. The horizontal 691 engine was mounted at the rear and was coupled to a six-speed ZF synchromesh gearbox. Moseley imported several right-hand drive coach versions which seated 53 passengers in an overall length of 38ft, the first arriving in 1972. Luggage lockers were provided under the floor between the axles giving more space than that lost to the engine. Few were sold possibly due to having a higher unladen weight than competitive conventional coaches with the penalty of higher fuel consumption and the British operators' reluctance to accept what had been used in many parts of the world for decades — chassisless construction.

Above: *Strachan built the 54-seat bodies on the six Swifts bought by Wolverhampton Corporation in 1967. They were amongst the fleet that passed to the West Midlands PTE on 1 October, 1969. They did not have a very long life with the PTE, being withdrawn between 1972 and 1974. The two sold in 1972 went to Northampton Corporation.* Ian Allan Library

Right: *St Helens Corporation was absorbed into the Merseyside PTE on 1 April 1974. By that time 66 Swifts with AH505 engines were in operation, all but three having 33ft long Marshall dual door bodies. The others by Alexander were ex-LUT. Illustrated is the first of the second batch which totalled nine vehicles; these were delivered in 1968 and seated 44. In 1975 a further nine Swift/ Marshall buses arrived having been ordered by St Helens.* Author's Collection

Above: *The last Swifts to enter service were a pair in 1976 for Grimsby Cleethorpes with East Lancs 43-seat dual purpose bodies. They had AH505 engines and were 33ft long.* G. H. Truran

Right: *London Transport used the name Merlin for both its AH691 and AH505 powered Swifts. Altogether 665 were bought but they did not prove to be as reliable as other AEC designs. Sold when only eight years old, this pair was one of over 110 bought by Ulsterbus. Although these are operating in Belfast they wear different liveries — the one on the right being Citybus.* W. Montgomery

Left: *AEC developed a new engine in the mid-1960s which was intended for high performance long distance operation particularly suited for motorway cruising. The V8 was initially fitted into goods chassis but the 1970 Commercial Show featured a rear-engined coach chassis with this unit which developed 250bhp. Unfortunately the promise of the prototype engines did not show up in production and the Sabre remained unique, as did the ECW coach body.* Ian Allan Library

15 Associated Engineering

Whilst you will be familiar with the bus building activities of Midland 'Red', not so many may be aware that Northern General also built some buses and coaches in the mid-1930s. Their general manager — Donald Sinclair (later General Manager of Midland Red) — designed a three-axled chassis with a side engine like the Q but using an American 6.3litre six-cylinder petrol engine which was not as tall as the AEC engines. This allowed a lower floor level to be achieved with a seating capacity of 44 — a valuable asset as low bridges precluded the use of double-deckers on many busy routes. Whilst Northern General had built the first batch starting in 1933, AEC built 31 in 1935, six of which received 28-seat coach bodies. In 1938 when NGT built another batch themselves, as two-axled chassis, they used the more compact AEC 6.6litre engine that had been introduced in the Regal Mk II which they were already operating. These vehicles were 27ft 6in long and accommodated 40 passengers.

When the C&U regulations allowed 30ft long two-axled chassis from June 1950, NGT decided to build its own maximum length vehicles whilst waiting for the underfloor-engined chassis to prove themselves. The Company chose the Regal Mk I that it had bought in 1937/8 as the basis of these machines. Surprisingly the first 10 arrived as 35-seat coaches in 1951. These and all subsequent AEC-NGT rebuilds were 8ft wide and bodied by a small coachbuilder (Picktree) at Chester-le-Street, Co Durham. The eleventh chassis received a 43-seat bus body which was built to an austere specification to make the bus as light as possible. Whilst it had a half cab with the chromium plated radiator of the Regal Mk II the body resembled a product of the 1920s with a curved roof of slatted construction which was unlined. In 1953 12 more entered service. In 1952 11 more coaches were delivered with three more in 1953. These gave between seven and 10 years service. The Northern General and associated fleets also placed in service other coaches incorporating components from prewar AEC chassis. Built by J. C. Beadle, they were 30ft long full-fronted coaches seating 35, of chassisless construction. Ten delivered in 1953 were withdrawn seven years later and replaced with underfloor-engined coaches seating two more.

Another operator to purchase similar coaches was

Maidstone and District with a prototype arriving in 1950 and 40 more in 1951/2 using prewar Regent components. In 1955 23 postwar Regal IIIs new in 1948/9 were used in new coaches accommodating 37 with central entrances.

Another operator to rebuild chassis was Hanson of Huddersfield. Having bought many Regal Mk III buses in the early postwar period, these became obsolete with the advent of the underfloor-engined chassis. They were far from being worn out so several were rebuilt as double-deckers and when bodied with new Roe bodies, they started a useful second life.

One surprising operator to rebuild AECs was the Lincolnshire Road Car Co Ltd who placed two 30ft single deckers in service in 1951. Lincolnshire had bought very few AECs but in 1950 they took over Enterprise and Silver Dawn from Scunthorpe who had a mainly AEC fleet. Two of their prewar Regals were the candidates.

These are but a few examples of AEC engineering being used for a second life.

Below: In 1935 AEC built 26 three-axled chassis to the design of Northern General Transport. These had a side mounted American built petrol engine. Six of these received Short 28-seat coach bodies and the remainder 44-seat bus bodies. The coaches originally had canvas roofs but they were rebuilt in 1939 as seen. N. J. Treacher

Above: *In 1950 Northern General built some buses to the newly introduced 30ft length. This time it used 1937 AEC Regal I as the basis, extending the wheelbase and sending them to a small coachbuilder — Picktree which built an austere 43-seat bus body.* A. Taylor Collection

Left: *J. C. Beadle Ltd of Dartford, Kent an enterprising bodybuilder which developed a range of chassisless designs using lightweight and medium weight power units. Many operators had vehicles in good mechanical order which needed new bodies. In 1950 it launched a new coach to the new 30ft overall length into which they built the front and rear half of the old chassis. Maidstone and District sent 23 Regal Mk III chassis with 7.7litre engines to Beadle in 1955. They emerged in 1955/6 as extremely smart 37-seat coaches giving another eight or nine years' work.* N. J. Treacher

Below left: *Hansons Buses Ltd, and its associated haulage company were loyal AEC customers for many years. Having bought several 27ft 6in long Regal IIIs in the early postwar years, they decided to rebuild several of them, starting in 1957 when one was converted into a double decker. Other conversions followed with some chassis like this 1962 example being extended to 30ft and rebodied by Roe with 39-seat bus bodies.* 797 Preservation Group

16 Badge Engineering and Miscellania

One of the earliest cases of 'badge engineering' occurred in 1912 when an agreement was entered into for Daimler to sell surplus AEC production. These were the Y-type fitted with a similar-shaped radiator to the AEC but having 'Daimler' in script on the top tank. The arrangement ceased when the War Department became the prime customer from 1916 for all AEC's output.

With the possible reduction in sales in the postwar world due to the Government's plans for the nationalisation of passenger and goods transport, AEC joined with Crossley Motors Ltd of Stockport and Maudslay Motor Co Ltd, of Alcester, Warwickshire to form Associated Commercial Vehicles Ltd (ACV) in 1948 to reduce chassis costs by virtue of greater volume. The production at Stockport was concentrated on passenger vehicle bodywork from 1951 and the Maudslay factory produced special chassis using AEC components. Amongst these were a shortened Regent Mk III chassis with a 13ft 6in wheelbase for Merryweather who fitted various types of bodywork for use as fire appliances. They also built 10 Regent Mk III chassis for their local corporation — Coventry — in 1951, and eight Regal Mk IVs. The

names however did not entirely disappear as several examples of each 'make' appeared at the 1950 and several subsequent commercial motor shows. These shows were organised by the SMM&T who had strict rules, one of which limited the number of chassis of any one make that could be exhibited. By using Crossley and Maudslay names AEC could treble its allocation, and have three stands. Many of these vehicles reverted to AECs when they entered service.

Darwen Corporation, who had had some Crossleys in the early postwar years did purchase Crossley Reliance and Regent chassis — the last a Regent arriving in 1957 and which has now been preserved since withdrawal in 1977. Crossley was also responsible for the development of the chassisless Bridgemaster and the first three were delivered as Crossley Bridgemasters, before production was transferred to Park Royal, with the closure of the Errwood Park Works.

Whilst AEC discontinued using Crossley and Maudslay variants in the late 1950s apart from the Maudslay name on goods vehicles for the GPO, 'badge engineering' was used on their products when they joined the Leyland Group as the corporate identity for export vehicles decreed they were all called 'Leylands'.

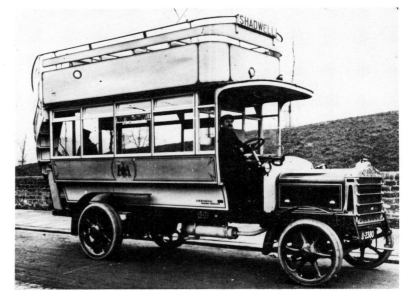

Right: An early example of badge engineering occurred in AEC's early years when surplus production was sold by Daimler. The 40hp example was the fifth bus to be bought by Leeds Corporation. Arriving in 1913, it has a 34-seat open-top double-deck body. In 1916 this Daimler was converted into a tower wagon for use on the tram and trolleybus overhead wires (Leeds and Bradford were pioneers, opening systems in 1911), a function it performed until December 1925. It was later scrapped. Author's Collection

Right: *Darwen Corporation (now part of Blackburn) bought some genuine Crossley double-deckers after the war. When manufacture had ceased in 1952, it bought some Reliances and a Regent as Crossleys. Entering service in 1957 with an East Lancs body, it was acquired for preservation when it finished service in 1977.* R. N. Hannay

Below right: *This Mandator began life as a petrol tanker for the Texas Oil Company in 1934. It was acquired by Gosport and Fareham in 1944 and fitted with a 7.7litre engine after being converted from normal to forward control and having a dropped rear frame extension. It was then bodied by Reading as a 56-seat highbridge bus. When withdrawn in 1960, the body had another four years of life on a 1947 Regent II chassis.* N. J. Treacher

Left: *As the Mandator was the prewar lorry equivalent of the Regent, so the Ranger was the passenger version of the Mercury lorry. Whilst it was sold in large numbers overseas, the Ranger was bought by a British firm in 1958 and bodied by Harrington. It was used on a service from London to Bombay in India. The passengers slept in tents for overnight stops — these being carried in the trailer.* Ian Allan Library

Right: *There were eight Regal Mk IV chassis which were registered as Maudslays and had and M prefix to their chassis numbers. This example has a Harrington coach body with only 33 seats and was built in 1951 — for a Birmingham operator.* Author's Collection